Set design by Peter Hicks   *Photo by Greg Mooney*

Trezana Beverley, Naima Carter Russell and Chinai J. Hardy in the Alabama Shakespeare Festival production of *The Nacirema Society Requests the Honor of Your Presence at a Celebration of Their First One Hundred Years.*

THE NACIREMA SOCIETY REQUESTS THE HONOR OF YOUR PRESENCE AT A CELEBRATION OF THEIR FIRST ONE HUNDRED YEARS

BY PEARL CLEAGE

★

DRAMATISTS
PLAY SERVICE
INC.

THE NACIREMA SOCIETY REQUESTS THE HONOR OF YOUR PRESENCE
AT A CELEBRATION OF THEIR FIRST ONE HUNDRED YEARS
Copyright © 2013, Pearl Cleage

SPECIAL NOTE

SPECIAL NOTE ON SONGS AND RECORDINGS

THE NACIREMA SOCIETY REQUESTS THE HONOR OF YOUR PRESENCE AT A CELEBRATION OF THEIR FIRST ONE HUNDRED YEARS received its world premiere at the Alabama Shakespeare Festival in Montgomery, Alabama, opening on September 24, 2010, with co-producing partner the Alliance Theatre in Atlanta, Georgia. It was directed by Susan V. Booth. The cast was as follows:

GRACE .... Trazana Beverly
JANET .... Jasmine Guy
CATHERINE .... Andrea Frye
BOBBY .... Kevin Alan Daniels
MARIE .... Chinai J. Hardy
ALPHA .... Tonia Jackson
LILLIE .... Karan Kendrick
GRACIE .... Naima Carter Russell
JESSIE .... Neda Spears

CHARACTERS

GRACE DUBOSE DUNBAR, African American woman, age 60

GRACIE DUNBAR, her granddaughter, age 18

MARIE DUNBAR, her daughter-in-law, age 40

CATHERINE ADAMS GREEN, African American woman, age 65

BOBBY GREEN, her grandson, age 21

ALPHA CAMPBELL JACKSON, African American woman, age 40

LILLIE CAMPBELL JACKSON, her daughter, age 21

JANET LOGAN, African American woman, age 33

JESSIE ROBERTS, African American woman, age 45

TIME

December 1964.

PLACE

Montgomery, Alabama.

ACT ONE

Scene One: Sunday, late afternoon
Scene Two: Monday afternoon
Scene Three: Tuesday, early afternoon
Scene Four: Tuesday, later
Scene Five: Tuesday, later
Scene Six: Tuesday evening
Scene Seven: Wednesday, 3 A.M.

ACT TWO

Scene One: Thursday morning
Scene Two: Thursday afternoon
Scene Three: Thursday evening
Scene Four: Friday evening
Scene Five: Friday evening

SETTING

There are three main playing areas: the formal living room and the library at Grace's house and the kitchen at the more modest home of Alpha Campbell's late mother. Only Alpha and Lillie enter this kitchen. Grace's living room, the main playing area, is tastefully decorated with antiques that have been in her family for generations, as has this house. On the walls are formal portraits of several generations of well-dressed African Americans who look back at the camera with complete confidence in their own beauty and an absolute awareness of their place in the world. There are the usual furnishings — couch, chairs, coffee table, etc. Everything is lovingly polished to a permanent shine.

There is a short stairway up to the library, which has floor-to-ceiling bookshelves, several leather chairs, a desk, a standing globe, etc. There are open books around and the room seems cozy and well used. There is one formal portrait in this room of a very handsome man dressed in white tie and tails. This is the late Dr. Louis Dunbar. His presence seems to dominate the room. There is a window. Also off the living room are a stairway exit to the unseen second floor of the house and another exit to a short hallway leading to the front door. This door should be visible when lit as if through a scrim. It is always answered by the fully uniformed maid who greets guests and family, takes their coats and exits without ever speaking an audible word. Guests ring the bell. The family doesn't ring a bell, but the maid somehow knows when they arrive and is always there to admit them. Jessie is a constant, albeit silent, participant in almost every scene; bringing coffee, refreshing sherry glasses, removing props, etc. Her active presence allows for scene changes to move quickly without the need for a total blackout since the audience can see her clearing up without taking them out of the play's real time.

When entering Grace's home, it is important to remember that even in the midst of massive social upheaval and revolutionary change, people still found time to fall in and out of love, to keep the family secrets or spill the beans and to embrace the great human chaos of their very specific lives. Fifty-four miles up the road from Montgomery in Selma, Alabama, plans are moving ahead for a massive voter education drive that will culminate at the foot of the Edmund Pettus Bridge on what came to be known as Bloody Sunday. In Oslo, Norway, the Nobel Committee has awarded the Peace Prize to Dr. Martin Luther King, Jr., but in Grace Dubose Dunbar's downstairs parlor, the focus is on the upcoming one hundredth anniversary celebration of the founding of The Nacirema Society, a post-slavery social organization, *for ladies only*, dedicated to the uplifting of young Negro womanhood.

THE NACIREMA SOCIETY REQUESTS THE HONOR OF YOUR PRESENCE AT A CELEBRATION OF THEIR FIRST ONE HUNDRED YEARS

ACT ONE

Scene 1

Lights up on Gracie Dunbar standing in the living room in a beautiful white ball gown. Her grandmother, Grace, is making one in a series of critical inspections of the dress. Her mother, Marie, is wiping down a Polaroid photo of the dress with the required developing agent. On the coffee table, there are a series of other photos of Gracie in various poses.

GRACE. Will you stand still?

GRACIE. I'm standing still! *(Grace raises her eyebrows.)*

MARIE. *(Trying to keep the peace.)* This one is lovely. *(Extends a photo toward Grace who ignores it.)*

GRACE. Turn! *(A command, not a request. Gracie obeys, but sighs loudly.)* There! Stop! *(She circles Gracie for a different view.)*

GRACIE. Do we have to do this now, Gram?

GRACE. When would you suggest we do it? If I don't get this dress back to Jennie by tomorrow morning, we'll never get it back in time. She hasn't even finished letting out Cheryl Harvey's bodice and she's still got Sandra Hoffman's sleeves to shorten. Cheryl's mother is beside herself, of course, even though she's partly to blame for letting that child eat the way she does. *Turn!*

9

GRACIE. It's fine, Gram. It fits perfect.

GRACE. Perfect*ly*, dear. *Perfectly.*

GRACIE. It fits *perfectly*, Gram.

GRACE. I'm a little concerned about the neckline. A small glimpse of décolleté is fine, but you've gotten so busty, it's almost cleavage and that will never do.

GRACIE. *(Tugs at the dress impatiently.)* Maybe I'm just wearing the wrong bra.

GRACE. *(Ignoring this completely.)* Do your curtsy. *(Gracie does a perfunctory dip. Grace waits for the real thing.)*

GRACIE. *Mom* …

MARIE. It looks lovely, sweetie. Just a few more minutes …

GRACE. A few more minutes? What is the point of doing all this hard work and planning if your dress looks like we just ran up a couple of croaker sacks and sent you out the door?

GRACIE. I just can't get as excited as you do about it, Gram. At the end of the day, it's just a big ol' poofy white dress.

GRACE. *(A beat.)* A Nacirema white is no ordinary ball gown. There are only six of them in the world, designed and hand stitched by Jennie Turner fifty years ago and lovingly altered by her to fit each new debutante in each subsequent year.

MARIE. She didn't mean anything by that, Grace. It's just getting so late and … *(A look from Grace silences Marie. Gracie is on her own.)*

GRACE. The Nacirema white is the essence of our tradition. It must not be simply perfect, but a standard of perfection, an unwavering beacon of light in a world of darkness. The Nacirema white, including this one, reminds us of why those two brave colored women — your great, great, great grandmother and Bobby's Green's great, great, great grandmother — stood there one hundred years ago in the ashes of everything they had ever known, clutching their baby girls and scratching out the words that you, as debutante of our centennial year, should know as well as you know your own name.

GRACIE. I do, Gram.

GRACE. Then say them.

GRACIE. *We do hereby found The Nacirema Society in order to uplift ourselves as free Negro women and to guide our daughters on the path of honor, chastity and truth.*

GRACE. So I don't think it's too much to ask that we take as much time as we need to make sure every Nacirema white reflects that intention.

GRACIE. Yes, ma'am. *(She executes a perfect curtsy.)*

MARIE. Beautiful! *(She takes another photo.)*

GRACE. See, right there on the left? There's just a little too much *round* for my taste.

GRACIE. *(She can't resist agitating her grandmother a little just for the fun of it.)* My anthropology teacher said some indigenous people won't let you photograph them. They think you're stealing their spirits.

GRACE. People indigenous to Alabama know better. *Walk!*

GRACIE. Gram! I swear the world could come to an end and if it wasn't on the society pages of *The Montgomery Advertiser* ...

GRACE. Don't say, *I swear,* darling. It's so low class. *Walk! (Grace and Marie watch her intently.)*

MARIE. Maybe it is just a little bit ... *round.*

GRACE. There used to be lace all around the neckline, but it just got so old and delicate, all you had to do was breathe on it and *poof!* So Jenny took it all off, but it does leave the neckline a little bare. *Sit! (Marie pulls over a small chair and smiles at her daughter encouragingly. Gracie sits.)*

MARIE. Maybe you could ask her to ...

GRACE. ... and get my head snapped off? No, thank you! You see what I mean about the cleavage? There it is again.

MARIE. *(Suddenly sentimental.)* Our little girl is growing up.

GRACE. Growing up is fine. Busting out all over is not fine.

GRACIE. Are we almost done?

GRACE. How can you possibly have someplace to go? It's Sunday evening!

GRACIE. I told you, Gram, I'm interviewing a woman who was part of the maids' committee during the bus boycott.

GRACE. At six o'clock on Sunday night?

GRACIE. She lives in, Gram. Sunday is her only day off.

GRACE. What are you doing talking to such a person anyway?

GRACIE. She's not *such a person.* She's just a person.

GRACE. My question remains the same. *Turn!*

GRACIE. It's for my senior project.

GRACE. I thought you were doing your senior project on the history of The Nacirema Society.

GRACIE. It would give me an unfair advantage if I write about The Nacirema Society since I'm part of it.

GRACE. I thought that was the whole point.

GRACIE. Well, my teacher didn't see it that way so I'm doing an oral history instead. *(Dramatically, with a flourish.)* The Montgomery Bus Boycott Ten Years After: Lasting Change or Business as Usual?

MARIE. That sounds interesting.

GRACE. Interesting is not the word I'd use.

GRACIE. It's been ten years, Gram. Don't you want to know if it worked?

GRACE. They wanted to sit at the front of the bus. Now they can.

GRACIE. Now *we* can.

GRACE. I've never ridden a city bus in my life, so it's all relative isn't it?

GRACIE. Don't worry, Gram. The interview won't take that long, I promise.

GRACE. Where does this woman even live? Is it safe?

MARIE. I'm going to drive her, Grace. She'll be fine.

GRACE. You should get Joseph to take her.

GRACIE. No way! I'm not going to pull up to interview these people in a big old Lincoln with a chauffeur in a uniform!

MARIE. I thought I'd run by and check on Lillie's since it's just around the corner.

GRACE. Why on earth would you do that?

MARIE. Catherine called while you were out this afternoon and said when she went by to see Francine yesterday, the lights were on even though they've still got the "For Sale" sign out and nobody's supposed to be living there.

GRACE. I told Catherine there was no need for her to be hovering over the woman every other day. Doesn't Francine have family who can look in on her?

MARIE. Francine worked for the Greens for thirty years, Grace. I think it's entirely appropriate that Catherine should visit her.

GRACE. Why didn't she just call the police about Lillie's?

MARIE. She called me.

GRACE. Suit yourself. *(Returning to the fitting.)* Wave your left arm. *Slowly. (Marie takes another shot, smiling encouragingly at Gracie.)*

GRACE. I'm sorry you're going out. I was hoping we could have supper together and catch up a little.

GRACIE. Catch up on what, Gram? We see each other every day.

GRACE. Just something a little bird told me about a certain person being engaged by Easter.

GRACIE. You can tell that little bird I wouldn't marry Bobby

Green if he was the last Negro on earth.

GRACE. He may not be the last one, but he certainly represents a dying breed.

GRACIE. He looked healthy enough last time I saw him.

GRACE. That's not what I mean and you know it. There are just so few young men around anymore who even know the basics. These girls we're reaching out to are challenging enough, but the escorts they're choosing? Impossible! We're going to have to start having classes. They need everything from basic etiquette to appropriate grooming and they've never even seen a waltz!

GRACIE. Where would they?

GRACE. My point exactly.

GRACIE. Don't feel bad … *badly*, Gram. They do that for the Motown people, too.

GRACE. Do what?

GRACIE. Teach them what fork to use and stuff so that when they visit the Queen, they won't embarrass themselves.

GRACE. I hope somebody is going to teach them how to dress.

GRACIE. They already know how to dress, Gram. You've seen the Supremes. How classy can you get?

GRACE. Don't say *classy*, and those wigs are ridiculous.

GRACIE. *(Teasing.)* I'm going to get one. A great big one with bangs in the front and a *poof* on the top and a saucy little flip all around.

GRACE. I'll saucy you! Leave your hair just the way it is. *(Studying the photos of Gracie that Marie has arranged neatly on the table.)* And I don't care what you say, it would be a great feather in your cap to arrive on campus at Fisk with a beautiful engagement ring to show everybody you're already spoken for.

GRACIE. Do you ever listen to a word I say?

GRACE. No, dear, not if I can help it. Now let me see your waltz and I think we're done.

GRACIE. *(Groans.)* Mom!

MARIE. Come on, sweetie. I'll be Bobby. *(She strikes an exaggerated formal pose. Gracie giggles and moves into her mother's arms. They waltz under Grace's watchful eye.)*

GRACIE. Did you ever want to be part of it, Gram?

GRACE. Part of what?

GRACIE. The boycott.

GRACE. I was part of it.

GRACIE. Sending Granddaddy across town to pick up Lillie

13

doesn't count!

GRACE. Why doesn't it?

GRACIE. Because you were only doing it so there would be somebody here to cook our dinner. You just said you never even took a city bus!

GRACE. And that year was no different. Why minimize my contribution just because I was already, in effect, boycotting?

GRACIE. But you had other options!

GRACE. And so did they, once they chose to exercise them. Everybody got where they were going without the bus, just like we did.

GRACIE. A chauffeur doesn't count either!

GRACE. Don't be silly. A chauffeur always counts. But I'm through talking about the past! In less than a week, I will present my granddaughter and five of her friends to the crème de la crème of Negro Montgomery, and Arthur L. Freeman will be snapping pictures of us all as we smile and sip our champagne and carry forward the best of who we are. *(A beat.)* I couldn't be prouder of you.

GRACIE. I love you, Gram.

GRACE. I love you, too. *(A beat.)* All right! We're done. Go and get changed and hang that dress on the padded hanger on the back of my closet door. I'll take it over to Jennie first thing in the morning.

GRACIE. I will! *(She dashes upstairs, tugging at the dress.)*

GRACE. Marie, go help that child before she tears something and Jennie Turner will demand all our heads on a stick!

MARIE. Well, we can't have that! *(Heading for the stairs.)*

GRACE. And Marie? Make sure she uses the *padded* hanger, will you? And don't let her bunch up the hem in the garment bag. You know how she just stuffed it in there before.

MARIE. Stop worrying. You've been planning this since before Gracie was born. Nothing can mess it up. Not even you.

GRACE. Never say never. It's bad luck.

MARIE. I thought you didn't believe in luck.

GRACE. I don't, but why take a chance? *(Marie exits upstairs. Black.)*

14

Scene 2

Lights up on Alpha Campbell in her mother's kitchen. Unoccupied since her mother's death, several months before, the house still has many of Lillie Campbell's things in it, including a kitchen table and chairs, curtains at the back door window, a cookie jar and a corkboard for posting family reminders, grocery lists, etc. Alpha is in a bathrobe and slippers, maybe her mother's. She is pouring herself a cup of coffee. The newspaper is on the table. She sits down, glances at the front page, just thumbing through and stops suddenly at a photograph. She reaches into the robe pocket, gets her glasses, puts them on and reads. When she finishes, she goes to one of the kitchen drawers, takes out a pair of scissors, clips the article carefully and then pins it in the center of the corkboard. She stands looking at it for a minute then sits back down at the table, drinking her coffee, lost in thought.

Lights lower in the kitchen area as lights come up full on Grace at her desk in the library. She's writing in a small notebook as if making a list and checking it twice. When the doorbell rings, Jessie Roberts, the uniformed maid, goes to open it, admitting Catherine Green. Grace closes the notebook, leaves the library and goes downstairs. Catherine gives her coat to Jessie and comes into the living room to greet Grace who embraces her.

CATHERINE. Dearest ...
GRACE. Your cheek is like ice!
CATHERINE. It's so windy out there! I had to have Joseph walk me to your door or risk flying off like Mary Poppins! It feels more like February than December.
GRACE. How about a glass of sherry to take the chill off your bones?
CATHERINE. That would be lovely. *(Grace pours them each a small glass from a decanter on the sideboard.)*
GRACE. Well what brings you out on such a blustery afternoon

15

that you couldn't tell me on the phone?

CATHERINE. *(She puts down her glass slowly, suddenly almost childlike in her fear of incurring the wrath of a superior force.)* Don't be angry, Grace. Promise me.

GRACE. I can't be angry with you.

CATHERINE. *(A beat. She knows from experience this is not the whole truth.)* What else could I do, when you think about it? It's not New York where we could just check her into the Plaza hotel and be done with it.

GRACE. Calm down and tell me what you're talking about. I won't get angry.

CATHERINE. I talked to that reporter.

GRACE. Which reporter?

CATHERINE. The one who did that story in *The New York Times.*

GRACE. *(A beat.)* What did I say?

CATHERINE. I know but ...

GRACE. What did I say?

CATHERINE. You said you didn't want to talk to her anymore, but ...

GRACE. What did I say *exactly?*

CATHERINE. You said she was dead to you.

GRACE. So why are we talking about her?

CATHERINE. Because she's coming back.

GRACE. From the dead?

CATHERINE. She said she was sorry that what came out wasn't the piece she turned in. They edited it and she didn't even see that awful headline until she opened the morning paper just like we did.

GRACE. I don't believe that for one minute. "Out of Time and Out of Touch." Why did you even talk to her?

CATHERINE. Apparently, she's been trying to reach you and Jessie keeps taking the message, but you never call her back.

GRACE. Jessie has too much sense to bring me a message from a dead woman.

CATHERINE. Listen, Grace, I know you're still mad and you're right to be. We all feel the same way. That story made us look like a bunch of silly, social climbing fuddy duddies.

GRACE. Exactly. All she did was string together a bunch of non-sense from people without a refined bone in their bodies. There was nothing in that piece but a lot of rumor, speculation and jealousy.

CATHERINE. But that was not her intention. She's just a reporter.

Her editors have the last word on what actually goes in the paper.

GRACE. Then why did it have her name on it?

CATHERINE. The point is, she's sorry at how things turned out and she wants to make it up to us by doing another piece covering the cotillion. They're going to send a photographer and everything.

GRACE. From New York?

CATHERINE. Can't you just see little Gracie in her Nacirema white and my Bobby in his white tie and tails, right there on the society pages of *The New York Times*? *(The enormity of the idea is dawning on Grace and she is warming to it.)* This is what we've dreamed of, Grace. This is what we've been working for all these years.

GRACE. If we're going to do this, everything has to be perfect.

CATHERINE. And it will be. *(Quickly.)* That's why she has to stay here with you.

GRACE. Now you have lost your mind!

CATHERINE. Where would you suggest she stay? The Ben Moore Hotel is already booked up for the holidays. Are you going to send her all the way to Birmingham to camp out at Mr. Gaston's Motel?

GRACE. She was dead to me two minutes ago, now she's my houseguest?

CATHERINE. You're our *doyenne*. Who else can host her appropriately? Who else can showcase the absolute best of who we are?

GRACE. Well, I guess you've got a point there.

CATHERINE. Good! Then it's settled. I'll call her when I get home and let her know you'll be looking for her tomorrow afternoon.

GRACE. Tomorrow? Why is she coming three days early?

CATHERINE. She said she wants to get it right this time. She wants to talk to some of our people, especially you, if you will allow it. She wants to set the record straight. That's what she said, Grace. They want to set the record straight.

GRACE. And just think, it only took them one hundred years.

CATHERINE. Grace, I really wish you'd try to get into the spirit of this. She seems like a lovely young woman and she must be good at her job. How many Negroes do you think get to work at *The New York Times* anyway?

GRACE. Spare me. She was pushy and rude and condescending and inappropriate. I don't care if it is *The New York Times*. *(A beat.)* But I guess that's neither here nor there at this point, is it?

CATHERINE. *(Gently.)* No, dear. I don't suppose it is.

GRACE. Then I think we should have a toast. *(She refills their glass-*

es.) To the one hundredth anniversary of The Nacirema Society.

CATHERINE. And to our beloved founders.

GRACE. Honor.

CATHERINE. Chastity.

BOTH. And truth. *(They clink and drink.)*

CATHERINE. I never tire of this room, Grace. It's always the calm at the center of the storm.

GRACE. And we've seen our share!

CATHERINE. More than our share, but we survived them all, and now, my dear, dear, friend, here we sit, still strong.

GRACE. Did you ask Yvonne if John could stand in for Mr. Frazier if he can't get the time off?

CATHERINE. I did. She said he's ready to perform if called upon.

GRACE. He's a lifesaver! We've never had a debutante whose father was a factory worker with no time off for the cotillion.

CATHERINE. Can you imagine?

GRACE. You know when Gracie first asked us to look at Sarah Frazier for consideration, I just couldn't see it, but she's done so well. I'm proud of her.

CATHERINE. She is a lovely girl, but her background is just impossible.

GRACE. Times are changing all around us, Catherine. People don't care so much about those things anymore.

CATHERINE. People are wrong! Is there anything you need for me to do before Saturday? Everything is running so smoothly, I keep thinking we must be forgetting something.

GRACE. Not a thing. Joseph and I will pick up Dunbar's bust tomorrow. The flowers are ordered. Candles are cut with wicks trimmed. All menus have been finalized and approved. *No okra!*

CATHERINE. *(Wrinkling her nose.)* I don't know what that woman was thinking! Next thing you know, she'd have suggested we serve collard greens!

GRACE. Stop worrying. I've got it all under control.

CATHERINE. I do have one small concern, Grace, and I pass it on to you in case you haven't heard.

GRACE. Heard what?

CATHERINE. The rumblings in some quarters about demonstrations, boycotts, all that unpleasantness starting up again right over in Selma.

GRACE. Selma is fifty-four miles away and as far as I know, they have no cotillion planned for Saturday night, unless Dr. King has organized one himself.

CATHERINE. Isn't his wife from around there somewhere?

GRACE. She's from right up the road in Marion, which is why there's no excuse. He's from Atlanta, so what can you expect, but she knows better.

CATHERINE. Just the same, everybody's talking about it.

GRACE. Well, *everybody* should find a more constructive way to spend her time.

CATHERINE. *(Properly chastised.)* You're right, of course.

GRACE. *(Softening.)* I don't think much will come of it, but if they do start marching, it won't be anything we haven't been through before. Remember '55?

CATHERINE. How could I forget? Nobody could ride the buses and everybody was scrambling to get their maids to work on time.

GRACE. I was lucky. Dunbar wouldn't allow me to go out by myself so he had to pick Lillie up every morning and bring her to me before I'd even let him think about making his rounds.

CATHERINE. John refused to fetch Francine, no matter how much I begged him, so I finally had to get his big old blue Lincoln, the one he didn't like to drive, and go myself. When I got to her house, she came right out, but then I didn't know whether to tell her to get in the back or to sit up front beside me! I was a wreck!

GRACE. Remember when I had to organize a whole fleet of cars for cotillion night so that the waiters would be on time. Not to mention that temperamental chef we flew in from New Orleans that year.

CATHERINE. What were we thinking?

GRACE. I don't know, but by the time the dust cleared, there were six young women wearing Jennie's best Nacirema whites, waltzing beautifully in the arms of their very proud fathers.

CATHERINE. You outdid yourself, and this year will be no different.

GRACE. We'll give *The New York Times* a little peek at just how beautiful we really are.

CATHERINE. *(Gathering her things.)* Which is why I'm on my way to Dorothy's for a press and curl. *(She may pat her perfectly coiffed hair lightly.)* She's holding a space for you at three if you want it.

GRACE. Bless you! Tell her I'll take it.

CATHERINE. I will … *Oh!* I almost forgot. My Bobby got in late last night. I understand he plans to call on your granddaughter this afternoon.

GRACE. Wonderful! I know she's looking forward to seeing him.

CATHERINE. I know it's unwise to count our chickens, Grace, and I probably shouldn't have told the paper that they were already practically engaged, but I told Bobby point blank if he didn't marry Gracie, he could make his way in this world on his own wit and wisdom, not mine.

GRACE. If you keep threatening to write that boy out of your will, eventually you're going to have to do it.

CATHERINE. Don't worry, dear. I wouldn't do that to Gracie.

GRACE. Too bad this isn't India.

CATHERINE. What does India have to do with it?

GRACE. Arranged marriages are legal there. The family gets to decide who marries who. And when. *(Lights up on front door. Jessie opens the door without a bell ringing and admits Gracie who surrenders her coat.)*

CATHERINE. Very wise.

GRACE. One of the advantages of an ancient culture.

CATHERINE. Well, we're getting older by the day, dear, so I guess that's a blessing. *(Gracie enters the living room.)*

GRACE. Look who we conjured up!

GRACIE. Hello, Gram … *(Kisses Grace's cheek.)* Mrs. Green.

CATHERINE. Hello, dear! I'm so looking forward to seeing you in your Nacirema white. I'm sure you'll be a vision of loveliness.

GRACIE. Thank you.

CATHERINE. Bobby is a very lucky young man. You just be sure he knows it, will you?

GRACIE. Yes, ma'am.

CATHERINE. I'm embarrassing her, Grace! Look! How charming! No man can resist a blush like that! Did you see my car outside, dear? I told Joseph to be back at one o'clock sharp!

GRACIE. Yes, ma'am. He's parked right out front. *(Lights up on Jessie at the door.)* Jessie is waiting with your coat.

CATHERINE. Has the wind died down any?

GRACIE. Yes, ma'am.

CATHERINE. Lovely! Goodbye then! I'll tell Dorothy to expect you later. *(She takes her coat from Jessie and exits.)*

GRACE. Should I ask Jessie to set another place for lunch?

GRACIE. I'm not hungry. *(She's thumbing excitedly through her notebook.)* I had another interview for my project. Listen to this ...

GRACE. I wish you would forgo this nonsense until after the cotillion. It's too distracting.

GRACIE. I can't, Gram. All these people work so I have to make appointments based on their schedules, not mine.

GRACE. What are they, Rockefellers? With schedules and appointments? Deliver me!

GRACIE. I want to read you something. Here it is! Listen. *"If you're gonna call it real change ... "*

GRACE. One moment, please! To whom am I lending my ear?

GRACIE. Mrs. Daisy Ann Brown. She helped coordinate transportation so everybody could get to work. Listen to what she told me: *"If you're gonna call it real change, something has to happen besides where you get to sit on the bus. Otherwise, we're just riding up front on our way to clean the same white folks' toilets and wash the same white folks' dirty drawers."* (*Gracie is transported by the earthiness of the comment.*) That's what she said: *white folks' dirty drawers.*

GRACE. The woman seems to have a rather unattractive fixation on the more intimate aspects of her employer's lives.

GRACIE. It's an oral history, Gram. The whole point is to write down exactly what the people say.

GRACE. I think it's a waste of your time and my money.

GRACIE. Do you think what she's saying is true?

GRACE. Of course not. Things are changing every day. For example, we made history this very afternoon.

GRACIE. Who? Me and you?

GRACE. You and I. *The New York Times* is going to cover the cotillion.

GRACIE. (*Genuinely surprised.*) Our cotillion?

GRACE. Yes, my darling, just like I always knew they would once they stopped treating stories of Negro society as if some particularly gifted chimpanzees had learned to play Chopin. This is the beginning of a new day. Before long, you girls and your beaus will announce your engagements and your weddings and the christenings of your children in the pages of the same *Advertiser* that Governor Wallace's wife turns to in the morning with her soft boiled eggs and grits.

GRACIE. I don't care about Mrs. Wallace's eggs, Gram. Who is going to do the story for *The Times?*

GRACE. The same young woman who did that awful piece where

she only talked to the wild-eyed radicals. I can't remember her name. I've repressed it.

GRACIE. *(Delighted and awed.)* Janet Logan is coming back?

GRACE. Arriving tomorrow. She swears her editors ruined her good intentions and she wants to make it up to me. Catherine seems to believe her so she'll be spending a few days with us here at the house.

GRACIE. Janet Logan is going to stay *here?*

GRACE. Unless you have some objections.

GRACIE. Objections? She's my favorite reporter in the whole paper. Not that story about us, of course, but she's a wonderful writer, Gram. My journalism teacher thinks she might win the Pulitzer for her work on the Civil Rights movement.

GRACE. Then you be sure and make *Miss Might Win the Pulitzer* feel welcome and we'll let bygones be bygones. *(Bell rings. Jessie admits Bobby Green.)* That's probably Bobby Green. His grandmother said he got in very late last night and he's already knocking on your door. What did I tell you?

GRACIE. I've got work to do.

GRACE. You've got company. *(Enter Bobby Green.)* Well, you're a sight for sore eyes.

BOBBY. Hello, Mrs. Dunbar. Gracie …

GRACIE. Hey.

GRACE. Have you been practicing for that first waltz? You know I'm counting on you, Bobby.

BOBBY. I'm ready, Mrs. Dunbar.

GRACE. How are your classes going?

BOBBY. Fine, Mrs. Dunbar. I got high marks on all my final exams.

GRACE. High marks. Do you hear that, Gracie?

GRACIE. Congratulations.

BOBBY. Thank you.

GRACE. Well, keep up the good work, dear. I'll leave you two to do your catching up.

BOBBY. Always good to see you, Mrs. Dunbar.

GRACE. I'm very proud of you, Bobby. You know Dr. Dunbar always thought you had the makings of a first class physician.

BOBBY. I'll do my best, Mrs. Dunbar.

GRACE. I know you will. *(She exits. Gracie grins at him.)*

GRACIE. *(Mimicking him.)* Hello, Mrs. Dunbar. Nice day, Mrs.

22

Dunbar. You're looking lovely, Mrs. Dunbar. I'll do my best, Mrs. Dunbar.

BOBBY. I was just being polite.

GRACIE. I think it's a reflex. You see a grandmother, any grandmother, and you pucker up.

BOBBY. You're going to feel bad for being so mean when you see what I brought you.

GRACIE. It's too early for Christmas presents. We don't even have our tree up yet.

BOBBY. A small token in honor of your upcoming coming out party.

GRACIE. Go to hell. *(She takes the offering; a pair of chopsticks tied with a bow.)* What is this?

BOBBY. Chopsticks, my countrified friend, to remind you that there is life beyond Montgomery. They're opening a Chinese restaurant a block from the Fisk campus. You can practice with these so you won't embarrass me the first time I take you there.

GRACIE. *(Pleased.)* This is actually a pretty cool gift. It isn't worthy of you, or you're not worthy of it.

BOBBY. A simple thank you will suffice. How you been, kid? I hear we're practically engaged.

GRACIE. Did you see yesterday's paper? They're already planning the announcement party!

BOBBY. Did I at least give you a nice ring?

GRACIE. It's not funny. I wish they would just relax.

BOBBY. The one thing of which they are incapable. *(A beat.)* You know that last story you sent me was pretty good.

GRACIE. You liked it?

BOBBY. Yeah, I did. You surprise me, kid. You might be a writer one day after all.

GRACIE. Was it too morbid?

BOBBY. It was a little messy, but not too much. Sounded like real people. Too bad you can't publish it.

GRACIE. Why not?

BOBBY. Because your grandmother will kill you.

GRACIE. If I'm really going to be a serious writer, I can't worry about things like that.

BOBBY. How are you going to be a writer without a patron?

GRACIE. I'll get a job. I'll have life experiences.

BOBBY. Writers don't need life experiences. They need imagination.

GRACIE. Do you believe that?

BOBBY. I think so. *(He grins at her.)* You look great.

GRACIE. Thanks.

BOBBY. Maybe we shouldn't dismiss this engagement thing right away.

GRACIE. And why is that? *(They've been flirting since they hit puberty and they're good at it.)*

BOBBY. Well, one good thing would be once we're engaged, I won't have to waste time in pursuit of sex.

GRACIE. How do you figure?

BOBBY. Because I'll have you. Once we get engaged, we'll be doing it on the regular.

GRACIE. Who told you that?

BOBBY. Your grandmother.

GRACIE. She did not!

BOBBY. Not in so many words, but I'll bet if you ask her, she'd tell you to indulge me.

GRACIE. I thought you were madly in love with some mystery woman from the north.

BOBBY. *(A beat.)* Things didn't work out. I'm back on the market. Rock bottom prices, too.

GRACIE. What happened? You spent two months in rural Mississippi with her last summer, for god's sake! I thought you said you were soul mates.

BOBBY. My grandmother doesn't believe in soul mates.

GRACIE. What does that mean?

BOBBY. It means I'm not ready to get married yet, no matter what you read in the papers!

GRACIE. Fine with me. I'm going to New York City and be a serious writer. I'm not interested in being anybody's wife.

BOBBY. You could be my mistress. Isn't that what serious writers do?

GRACIE. Not if they have any sense, they don't. I'm starving! Can we please go get something to eat so I can try out my new chopsticks?

BOBBY. There aren't any Chinese restaurants around here.

GRACIE. Is there a law that says I can't use them on collard greens?

BOBBY. If I feed you, can we go somewhere and make out afterward?

GRACIE. Why are you so lame?

BOBBY. Why are you so fine?

GRACIE. Stop trying to distract me with your dazzling charms and tell me what happened to your soul mate. *(She links her arm through his.)*

BOBBY. You think I'm dazzling?

GRACIE. You have your moments. *(They exit. Black.)*

Scene 3

Lights up on Alpha Campbell in a well-cut dark suit. She enters the kitchen carrying two handbags. She dumps out the contents of one on the table and begins to replace items in the empty bag. The bag contains: a souvenir handkerchief that says "New York City"; a cosmetics bag; a small notebook; several pens; a pack of Doublemint gum; a wallet and a small copy of The New Testament. The purse she's transferring into is a small black envelope bag with room for essentials only so she's choosing carefully.

Alpha is startled by the sound of a key in the back door. Enter Lillie Campbell, her daughter. Lillie is dressed in overalls and boots, a turtleneck sweater and a navy pea jacket. She has a well-worn backpack slung over her shoulder and she looks weary. Her hair is worn in a natural style. Each is amazed to see the other.

ALPHA. Lillie!?

LILLIE. Mom!?

ALPHA. What are you doing here?

LILLIE. What are *you* doing here? *(During the following exchange, both women are lying so they may hesitate or stumble over a word or two as they spin their stories.)*

ALPHA. I'm here to handle some business with Grandmom's house. You know, the sale and everything?

LILLIE. Did they find a buyer?

ALPHA. Not yet and it's been six months. I thought maybe they needed to see my face in the place. Now your turn.

LILLIE. I'm meeting a friend from school. She's going to ride with me to Greenwood after she takes her finals.

ALPHA. What happened to Prince Charming?

LILLIE. He can't go. He's has to ... study.

ALPHA. I guess he figures Mississippi is a lot more civilized than it was last summer and you can look out for yourself this time? Chivalry is not what it used to be!

LILLIE. He's not required to go every time I go.

ALPHA. Of course he is. What good is Prince Charming if he doesn't stand between you and the dragon?

LILLIE. Don't you mean the grand dragon?

ALPHA. That's not funny.

LILLIE. Don't get all worked up. It doesn't matter if he does or doesn't. I'm going.

ALPHA. You get that stubbornness from your father.

LILLIE. And my good looks from you. *(Kisses Alpha.)*

ALPHA. But not your sense of style. Are the overalls absolutely necessary?

LILLIE. Practically required. Where are you going all dressed up anyway?

ALPHA. *(Evasive.)* I told you. I've got an appointment with a lawyer. *(Tosses the rest of her things in her purse.)* About ... the house. Just some business, you know. How long were you planning to be here?

LILLIE. I'm not sure. My ... friend hasn't finished her exams yet, but I don't have to be in Greenwood until Saturday, so ... I thought I'd stay here instead of just knocking around the campus since everybody's gone home for Christmas break.

ALPHA. I didn't even know you had a key to this place.

LILLIE. Grandma gave it to me when we were arguing so much the summer of my senior year. She said even if I never needed it, she wanted me to know I had options.

ALPHA. Was I that bad?

LILLIE. This is the first time I've ever used it.

ALPHA. And this time it doesn't have anything to do with me, right?

LILLIE. Not a thing.

ALPHA. *Good!* Then go upstairs and put your stuff in my old room. I made up that bed and you can bunk with me. There are clean towels in the bathroom if you want a shower and I'll be back before you know it. Got plans for dinner?

LILLIE. Thelma's, if she's still around.

ALPHA. As long as there are colored folks within a fifty mile radius, Thelma's will always be around. *(Kisses her.)* Go on and get cleaned up. You look beat.

LILLIE. I am exhausted.

ALPHA. *(Stops at the door.)* I'm glad you're here.

LILLIE. Me, too.

ALPHA. Gives me a couple of more days to try to talk you out of that Mississippi madness.

LILLIE. A small price to pay for Thelma's mac and cheese.

ALPHA. *(Laughing.)* I'm late! Gotta go! *(Grabs her coat from the back of the chair.)* See you later, alligator! *(Alpha exits.)*

LILLIE. After awhile, crocodile! *(Lillie drops her pack and looks around. She sees the coffee on the counter and pours herself a cup, wrapping her hands around the warm mug, she leans against the counter. She has been in this room many times and it is filled with pleasant memories of the grandmother for whom she was named. Her eye suddenly falls on the bulletin board where her mother had pinned the newspaper clipping earlier. Lillie walks over to it with complete disbelief. She puts down her coffee, takes the clipping down, sits at the table with it in her hand, reading with growing amazement and confusion. When she finishes reading, she looks up slowly, unconsciously crumbling the clipping in her hand. Black.)*

Scene 4

Lights up on Marie sitting on the couch in the living room reading a typewritten manuscript intently. Gracie is sitting on the steps up to the library, her arms nervously clasped around her knees. Marie finishes the last page of the story, puts the pages down slowly, savoring the ending.

MARIE. You can come out now!

GRACIE. *(Jumps up and comes into the living room.)* Well?

MARIE. It's wonderful.

GRACIE. Really? I was so afraid you wouldn't like it!

MARIE. It's the best one you've ever written. No contest.

GRACIE. Were the others that bad?

MARIE. They were all good. This one is *wonderful.* Congratulations! *(Hands it back to her.)*

GRACIE. You'd tell me the truth if it was terrible, right?

MARIE. I'd have no choice. I'm your mother. It's against the rules for me to lie.

GRACIE. To anybody or just to me?

MARIE. Just to you. It's part of the maternal code.

GRACIE. Do you think Gram would kill me if she read it?

MARIE. Probably, but publishing is in the grey zone. We've never had a writer before.

GRACIE. Bobby said she would.

MARIE. Bobby may have exaggerated the risk just a little based on his experience with Catherine.

GRACIE. Do you think she'd kill me if I didn't go to Fisk?

MARIE. *(Still teasing.)* Absolutely. The rules are very clear about the appropriate punishment for breaking a family tradition.

GRACIE. I'm serious.

MARIE. What are you talking about? Of course you're going. You've got a full scholarship.

GRACIE. I got one to Barnard, too.

MARIE. In New York City?

GRACIE. I applied to the Creative Writing program. I sent this story. And they accepted me.

MARIE. *(Proud but concerned.)* Oh, baby! Why didn't you tell me?

GRACIE. I'm telling you now.

MARIE. Duboses and Dunbars have gone to Fisk since 1866. It means a lot to Grace.

GRACIE. If I want to be a serious writer, I have to go to New York.

MARIE. Can't you be a serious writer in Nashville?

GRACIE. *(A beat.)* No.

MARIE. *(A beat.)* Then I guess you better go to New York.

GRACIE. I knew you'd understand! *(They embrace. Bell rings. Jessie admits Alpha Campbell.)*

MARIE. You expecting company?

GRACIE. Not me. I've got homework. *(She heads for the stairs.)* Can you run me over to the library later?

MARIE. As long as we're back before dinner, and do me a favor, will you? Don't tell Gram about Barnard.

GRACIE. Why not?

MARIE. Your grandmother reacts more positively to things when she thinks they're her idea.

GRACIE. But this isn't her idea.

MARIE. By the time I'm done, it will be. *(Exit Gracie. Enter Alpha. Recognizes her immediately.)* Alpha Campbell? What a pleasant surprise. Marie Dunbar.

ALPHA. It's Alpha Campbell Jackson now. I didn't expect you to remember me.

MARIE. Of course I remember you. Lillie was a part of this family for forty years. She talked about you so often.

ALPHA. Yes, well, I guess that's what mothers do.

MARIE. Won't you sit down?

ALPHA. Thank you. I apologize for just barging in like this, but I have some … business to discuss with Mrs. Dunbar. The *other* Mrs. Dunbar.

MARIE. I'm sorry, she's been gone all morning. The cotillion is Saturday and she's making sure everything is as it should be. Was she expecting you?

ALPHA. No. I didn't have an appointment or anything. I'm in town on business and it seemed a good time to drop by.

MARIE. *(A realization.)* Are you staying at your mother's house?

ALPHA. *(Immediately wary.)* Yes. Why?

MARIE. A friend of Grace's saw the lights on the other night and was concerned about intruders because the place has been empty since … since your mother passed. I rode by last night to check on things, but you must have been out.

ALPHA. Yes, well … I'm sorry to have bothered you.

MARIE. You're welcome to wait. She should be back any minute now.

ALPHA. Are you sure I'm not imposing?

MARIE. Absolutely not. *(Pours two sherries.)* Would you like a glass of sherry?

ALPHA. Thanks. I don't believe I've ever actually had a glass of sherry.

MARIE. It's kind of sweet for my taste, but Grace thinks anything stronger is the first step on the road to ruin.

ALPHA. I've actually heard that road runs right through the middle of Montgomery.

MARIE. To first steps and open roads! *(They toast.)* I was trying to remember the last time I saw you. We were out of town for your mother's service.

ALPHA. So I heard.

MARIE. She was a wonderful woman. *(A beat.)* I think it was during the bus boycott. That's ten years ago!

ALPHA. I remember. I came home to check on my mother. All the news we were getting in New York looked pretty scary and I knew she'd be right in the thick of it.

MARIE. She sure was.

ALPHA. You had a daughter, didn't you?

MARIE. Gracie. She'll be eighteen next month. You have …

ALPHA. A daughter, too. Lillie. She's in her senior year at Fisk.

MARIE. Named after her grandmother just like mine.

ALPHA. She's here with me for a couple of days, but she's going to Meharry in the fall.

MARIE. Congratulations. I remember when girls went to Meharry to marry doctors. Now they *are* doctors!

ALPHA. It's a new world, Mrs. Dunbar. My daughter tells me that all the time.

MARIE. Mine does, too. Call me Marie.

ALPHA. *(Liking Marie in spite of herself.)* I'm Alpha.

MARIE. I didn't know your mother as well as I wish I had, but we had some times during the boycott.

ALPHA. Were you involved in it, too?

MARIE. Through no fault of my own! I gave your mother a ride one night after they had been walking for about a month or so. She was going to a meeting and she didn't want Grace to know, so she asked me to drop her at the First Baptist Church. Of course, I was glad to do it. All along the way, whenever she saw somebody she knew, walking, she'd ask me to stop and pick them up, so I did. By the time we got there, Grace's old Buick was stuffed to the gills and people were coming from all directions. It was January and cold, but everybody was so excited, they didn't even seem to notice. When we got there and everybody piled out, I asked your mother what was going on — my husband had just died and I wasn't really keeping up with anything except Gracie — so Lillie just smiled and said, *Dr. King is speaking,* and invited me to come in, so I did.

ALPHA. I've never heard him speak. He came to New York once, but I couldn't get in. People stood in line for hours. *(Enter Gracie from upstairs. She stops to listen, not wanting to break the spell of the*

30

story. She's carrying library books.)

MARIE. He wasn't the only one who spoke. There were some other ministers and some young people, but when they finally introduced him, it got so quiet. It was like everybody leaned forward and took a deep breath so they wouldn't have to take another one before he finished. *(A beat.)* He didn't speak long, but just listening to him made you feel brave! When he sat down, the whole place exploded. People were clapping and smiling and hugging each other and then the choir started singing "This Little Light of Mine." They didn't even have to change the words. It was already a freedom song and that's how we sang it, over and over, louder and louder, until all we heard was each other. *(A beat.)* After that, whenever your mother needed a ride to the rallies, I'd find a reason to borrow Grace's car and off we'd go.

GRACIE. You never told me you were involved in the bus boycott!

MARIE. You never asked me. Alpha Campbell Jackson, this is my daughter, Gracie.

ALPHA. Pleased to meet you.

GRACIE. Are you Miss Lillie's daughter?

ALPHA. Her one and only.

GRACIE. I knew your mother.

ALPHA. I know. She used to write me letters about how smart you were. *(Enter Grace. She gives her coat to Jessie without acknowledging her. As she heads for the living room, she hears Gracie and an unfamiliar voice. She listens.)*

GRACIE. She was the first person I ever let read my stories, other than my mom. She was always teasing me after that, calling me Mrs. Shakespeare.

ALPHA. She told me you were going to be a great writer like Langston Hughes.

GRACIE. I hope so. I'm going to New York in the fall — *(Grace enters the living room as if she has no idea anyone else is present. Marie instantly steps in to keep Grace from spilling the beans about Barnard.)*

MARIE. Grace, there you are!

GRACE. The bust is perfect! It's so lifelike I thought Dunbar was going to speak up and give his opinion, which would be so like him, wouldn't it?

MARIE. You've got company.

GRACE. *(She turns toward Alpha for the first time.)* Company?

ALPHA. Mrs. Dunbar …

31

GRACE. *(Unpleasantly surprised)* Is it Alpha? Alpha Campbell?

ALPHA. Alpha Campbell Jackson.

GRACE. Of course, you did marry, didn't you? How lovely to see you, and what a surprise!

ALPHA. I'm sure.

MARIE. Gracie and I are on our way to the library, so we'll leave you two, but I hope we'll see you again while you're in town.

ALPHA. Yes, but I'm not sure exactly when we're leaving.

MARIE. *(Impulsively.)* Why don't you and Lillie come to dinner on Friday? *(Grace is clearly not pleased with this idea, but Marie is oblivious.)* We're having a few friends over and I'd like for the girls to meet, especially since they'll both be in Nashville this fall.

GRACIE. We will?

MARIE. Alpha's daughter, Lillie, is going to Meharry. *And you'll be at Fisk.*

GRACIE. *(Remembers they have a secret from Grace.)* Oh, right! Fisk!

MARIE. Around seven-thirty?

GRACIE. Please come. There's going to be a reporter here from *The New York Times* to cover the cotillion.

MARIE. See? We've already got a crowd coming! Adding two more will be a breeze.

ALPHA. All right then, thank you. If we're still in town, we'll be here.

MARIE. Good.

GRACIE. See you on Friday. *(They exit. Grace and Alpha are alone. Grace is not sure why Alpha is there and Alpha is not sure how to open the subject of her visit. The pause is awkward.)*

GRACE. May I offer you a glass of sherry?

ALPHA. I already have one, thanks. *(Grace pours a glass for herself and sits down on the couch, impatient, but gracious, for the moment.)*

GRACE. Well, you've certainly caught me in the middle of the whirlwind. Our annual ball is on Saturday. We're giving the award to my late husband this year and there are just so many details to attend to … but I guess I don't have to tell you. I'm sure The Nacirema Cotillion was as much a part of your life growing up as it was of mine.

ALPHA. I saw the article in the paper.

GRACE. Yesterday? Wasn't that a lovely picture of Gracie and Bobby Green?

ALPHA. I saw that one, but I meant the one in *The New York*

Times a few weeks ago.

GRACE. *(A beat. Something in Alpha's tone puts her on high alert, but still gracious.)* The one in *The Advertiser* was much nicer.

ALPHA. I can see how you would feel that way.

GRACE. *(A beat.)* I'm struck by how much you look like your mother. We certainly miss her around here.

ALPHA. Thank you. She often spoke of how much she valued your friendship.

GRACE. I'm surprised to hear that. Your mother was a lovely woman, but it's not as if we were *friends*. I don't think we ever had what you would call a *private* conversation in all the years she worked for me. That was never the nature of our relationship.

ALPHA. *(Stung.)* I see. I must have misunderstood.

GRACE. No harm done. So how have you been, dear? Still living up there in New York? I don't know how you do it. Dr. Dunbar and I used to go every year and see a show, but everything moves so fast I'd come home exhausted every time. But that's not the part of New York you live in, is it?

ALPHA. Mrs. Dunbar, I'm not here on a social call.

GRACE. Oh. Then why are you here?

ALPHA. What I have to say may shock or surprise you, but I assure you that it is not my intention. My intention is simply to do the honorable thing and set the record straight.

GRACE. I have no idea what you're talking about.

ALPHA. Before my mother passed, she told me something she had never told another living soul, but first she made me promise to keep her secret.

GRACE. And are you here to break that promise?

ALPHA. Dr. Dunbar was my father.

GRACE. *(A beat.)* I beg your pardon?

ALPHA. I never intended to do anything about it, but then I saw the article in *The Times* about The Nacirema Society and how you were celebrating your one hundredth anniversary and part of it was honoring Dr. Dunbar and I just couldn't keep the secret any longer. I'm here to demand that you withdraw the award and cancel plans to honor Dr. Dunbar. It is a slap in my mother's face and in my face and in my daughter's face.

GRACE. This is outrageous! My husband was a fine and honorable man and unless you can provide me with proof of your accusations, I would ask that you leave my house and not return.

ALPHA. I have proof.

GRACE. What kind of proof?

ALPHA. I have my mother's word. That's good enough for me.

GRACE. *(Relieved.)* I don't mean to be rude, dear, but that won't stand up in a court of law.

ALPHA. That may be true, but it will play just fine in the court of public opinion.

GRACE. What do you mean?

ALPHA. I mean if you don't cancel your plans as I have requested, I will be forced to go the press and tell them everything.

GRACE. We can't cancel our plans. Invitations went out months ago. Everyone who's anyone will be there. The unveiling of the bust is the highlight of the evening. Even the *white* paper will be there to cover it. *The New York Times* is sending a photographer. What possible reason could we give for rearranging the entire program?

ALPHA. That's hardly the point, Mrs. Dunbar. The point is, the honor of my family is at stake.

GRACE. Your family? What about my family?

ALPHA. Would you prefer *our* family? *(A beat. Grace regroups.)*

GRACE. Even if it were true, *which it most certainly is not,* this is hardly the time …

ALPHA. Maybe I should come back later and talk to your friend from *The Times*.

GRACE. You're trying to blackmail me!

ALPHA. *Blackmail?* I'm talking about honor!

GRACE. You can call it honor if you want to, but I know better! *(She goes to the phone.)* I'm going to call the police and have you arrested! You're a disgrace to your mother's memory!

ALPHA. Arrested for what?

GRACE. I don't know what laws prevail in New York City, but blackmail is still illegal in the state of Alabama. *(She picks up the phone and begins to dial.)* You'll get ten years for this.

ALPHA. *(A little nervous for the first time.)* Wait a minute!

GRACE. You come into my home, threatening to scandalize my family, without a shred of proof to offer. For what am I waiting?

ALPHA. I have proof!

GRACE. *(Stops dialing.)* Other than your mother's deathbed confession?

ALPHA. I have a letter.

GRACE. *(Hangs up the phone slowly.)* What kind of letter?

ALPHA. From Dr. Dunbar. A letter that ... admits paternity and ... confesses great respect and ... affection for my mother.

GRACE. Let me see it.

ALPHA. I didn't bring it with me. I thought, given the circumstances, my word would be enough. *(Grace looks at Alpha, trying to decide if she's telling the truth. Unable to tell, she does the next best thing to buy herself some time; she bursts into tears which throws Alpha off completely.)*

GRACE. I'm sorry ... it's all just so ... so humiliating. To think they could have deceived me for — how old are you?

ALPHA. Thirty-nine.

GRACE. For forty years! It's just too much to bear. *(She falls back against the couch dramatically as if she is about to faint.)* Would you please pour me another sherry? I feel almost faint. *(Alpha does. Grace fans herself elaborately with a white lace handkerchief.)* Thank you, dear. *(She sips then hands the glass back to Alpha who puts it down on the coffee table.)* Like any wife, I would hate to believe that my husband strayed, but if he did so, I do not want his indiscretion to destroy my good name and the good name of my granddaughter, especially when she's about to announce her engagement. I love Catherine Green like a sister, but I couldn't ask her to let her grandson marry into our family in the midst of this kind of scandal.

ALPHA. I think how far this goes is up to you, Mrs. Dunbar.

GRACE. Yes, I understand that. *(A beat.)* Perhaps there is something else that would protect your family's honor and leave mine intact as well.

ALPHA. *(This is exactly where she wants this conversation to go, but she makes Grace wait a beat for her response.)* What do you mean?

GRACE. I know, this is about honor, but it's not just Dr. Dunbar's honor that will be tarnished if all of this ... unpleasantness ... made it into the papers. Your mother was always a highly respectable woman. Your story will change all that.

ALPHA. *(Grace has hit a nerve. Alpha does feel guilty about this aspect of what she is doing.)* I think my mother would trust me to do the right thing.

GRACE. But what about your daughter? Do you want to destroy any viable marriage prospects she has by covering her in shame?

ALPHA. Whoever marries my daughter will have sense enough to realize he's a very lucky man.

GRACE. And she can be a very lucky girl if we can let everybody's honor fend for itself and perhaps in the spirit of … of letting by-gones be bygones … I can come up with a way to … compensate you for your … pain and suffering. *(She looks at Alpha to get some reaction. A beat. Alpha looks right back.)* I think it's the honorable thing to do.

ALPHA. *(Relieved but playing it out.)* Well, if you put it that way, I might be prepared to discuss some kind of compensation.

GRACE. You will find that I am a generous woman who hates even the breath of scandal.

ALPHA. As am I. Not the generous part, I don't have anything to be generous with, but the part about wanting to avoid any *breath* of scandal.

GRACE. Good. I'm glad we agree on that. *(A beat. Neither one knows exactly what's supposed to happen now.)*

GRACE. Of course, I'd want … I'd want to have the letter.

ALPHA. What?

GRACE. The letter. You said you had a letter.

ALPHA. Oh, yes. The letter.

GRACE. I think it's only fair.

ALPHA. You mean that we should … make an exchange?

GRACE. Exactly. Would you like to bring it by tomorrow?

ALPHA. No, well … it's actually not here in Montgomery.

GRACE. *(Immediately suspicious again.)* Where is it?

ALPHA. It's back in New York. I'll have to get my … attorney to send it to me.

GRACE. How long will it take to get here?

ALPHA. Two or three days if I can get him to send it airmail.

GRACE. Good, because as much as I want to ease your … pain and suffering, we don't really have … a deal … until I have that letter in my hand.

ALPHA. The sooner the better, I say.

GRACE. And I agree. So shall we say…?

ALPHA. I'll bring it to dinner on Friday.

GRACE. Oh, yes. I'd forgotten you were coming. This all comes as such a shock. Forgive me! *(She leans back and closes her eyes.)* It's been so much to take in all at once.

ALPHA. *(Not sure what to do. A beat.)* I'll see myself out.

GRACE. Thank you, dear, and Miss Jackson? Do I have your promise? Not a word of this to anyone?

ALPHA. Not a whisper.

GRACE. In some ways, Montgomery is a very small town.

ALPHA. I understand.

GRACE. Good.

ALPHA. Is there anything else?

GRACE. I always respected your mother.

ALPHA. I always respected your husband. *(Alpha exits, taking her coat from Jessie at the door. Grace listens for the sound of the door closing, then gets up and dials the phone quickly.)*

GRACE. Mrs. Green, please. *(A beat.)* Catherine? You know that old rumor about Dunbar and Lillie? ... Yes, that's the one. ... Well, it just came knocking at the front door. With bells on. *(Black.)*

Scene 5

Lights up on Marie, Gracie and a newly arrived Janet Logan coming into the living room. Gracie is carrying a small suitcase. Janet Logan is conservatively but stylishly dressed in a well-cut pants suit. They have just entered and handed their coats to Jessie. Lights also up in the library where Grace is at her desk, fiddling with a small locked box. She opens the box with a key and takes out a folded letter written on a piece of lined paper as if torn from a legal pad. She reads it quickly, refolds it, puts it back in the box, closes the box without locking it and leaves it on her desk. She sits, thinking; stands up, paces a bit, still thinking. She may look at the portrait of Dr. Dunbar with a mixture of emotions from time to time. She should react to the sound of the folks entering downstairs and sit down quietly, unwilling to reveal herself yet, but listening.

GRACIE. I read all your stories. My teacher has a friend in New York and every week she sends me all the papers from the week before.

JANET. You read the paper a week after it comes out? Doesn't that put you a little behind the times?

GRACIE. *(Laughing.)* Don't worry, I read *The Advertiser* in be-

37

tween so if anything really terrible happens, I'll know, but those reporters down there don't write like you do.

MARIE. Gracie's a fan.

GRACIE. I remember the one where you interviewed the parents of some of the kids who went to Mississippi after those three civil rights workers disappeared.

MARIE. That was one of yours?

JANET. One of my better efforts, I think.

GRACIE. They all said they were worried sick, but they were really proud of their kids and wouldn't think of asking them to come home.

MARIE. Thank goodness Gracie was too young to go.

GRACIE. And too scared!

JANET. I'm always scared on a story. Comes with the territory.

GRACIE. You write like you're not afraid of anything.

JANET. That's just how good I am!

GRACIE. How did you…?

MARIE. Gracie! For goodness sakes, let Miss Logan get in the door before you start interrogating her.

GRACIE. I'm not interrogating. I'm just making pleasant conversation.

MARIE. Well, pleasant that bag on upstairs to the guest room and let Gram know we're back.

GRACIE. Uh, oh! *(Sotto voce.)* My Gram is still a little mad at you.

JANET. I'm sorry about that. I hope she'll give me an opportunity to explain.

MARIE. *(Raising her eyebrows at Gracie to clam up.)* I'm sure she's forgotten all about it by now. *(Gracie exits upstairs. In the library, Grace stands quietly and goes over to the door, listening. In the living room, Marie smiles at Janet uncomfortably.)* Please, have a seat.

JANET. I was hoping my explanation had helped get things back on track.

MARIE. It did. A little.

JANET. I was as shocked as she was when I saw how they had chopped up the story, but it was out of my hands by then. *(Grace slowly and silently makes her way halfway down the stairs so she can hear the conversation.)*

MARIE. *(A beat. She knows Jan is lying.)* You made us look ridiculous.

JANET. That was not my intention.

MARIE. You're too good a writer for me to believe that.

JANET. It wasn't entirely my fault, you know. I tried to get an

38

interview with Mrs. Dunbar. She wouldn't talk to me and she wouldn't let anybody else talk to me. The only people eager to tell me what they knew and how they felt about The Nacirema Society were people whose opinions ranged from — may I speak frankly?

MARIE. Please.

JANET. From mild amusement to downright loathing. *(Grace reacts to this with visible annoyance, but remains hidden.)*

MARIE. That's a little harsh, don't you think?

JANET. Is it? *(A beat. Marie's look carries a warning.)* Look, I sold my editor on the idea of doing this piece because I was truly fascinated. I'd never heard much about these societies until I saw a piece about your hundredth anniversary in *Jet* a couple of months ago. There's not a whole lot written about them in the mainstream press, and I thought I could do something really interesting. I assumed you people would talk to me — I'm *The New York Times,* right? — but nobody would even take my phone calls. I had to crawl back to New York with nothing but an expense report and a lot of nasty quotes from people who have some pretty strong feelings about your mother.

MARIE. Mother-in-law. I was married to her son. He died ten years ago.

JANET. I'm sorry. *(A beat.)* The truth is, I knew the piece was one sided. I told myself it was her fault for refusing to see me, but as soon as I saw it in print, I knew I hadn't done my job. The Nacirema Society deserves better, and I can *do* better. *(Grace, still unseen, smiles to herself. She is vindicated. Marie doesn't know whether she believes Janet or not.)* That's why I'm here, to make it right. *(Grace enters from the library steps and goes immediately to Janet, hand outstretched in greeting.)*

GRACE. I'm Grace Dunbar ... Miss Logan. Welcome to my home.

JANET. Thank you, I wanted to —

GRACE. *(Cuts her off.)* I'm afraid you've caught us at a very busy time. *(Gracie enters from upstairs.)*

JANET. Oh, yes, certainly.

GRACIE. Gram! There you are. We're back!

GRACE. I can see that. *(To Marie.)* Catherine is on her way here with a small crisis and I won't be able to meet the florist at four. Will you be a dear and run over there and check his final designs for the table bouquets? Tell him baby's breath is a garnish, not the main course.

MARIE. I'm on my way. *(To Janet.)* Would you like to ride with me? Take the scenic tour of Montgomery?

JANET. I was hoping I could get a few minutes with you, Mrs. Dunbar. I know you don't have time for an interview, but maybe I could just be a fly on the wall.

GRACE. A fly on the wall?

JANET. I'd love to sit in on your meeting with Mrs. Green. Sort of a moment behind the scenes.

GRACE. Who told you I was meeting with Mrs. Green?

MARIE. You did, Grace. That's why I'm going to the florist.

GRACE. Oh, yes! My goodness. I've got so much on my mind. *(A beat.)* Why are you still here?

MARIE. I'm not! *(Bell rings. Jessie admits Catherine Green in a big rush. She greets Marie, who passes her as she exits.)*

GRACE. There she is now!

GRACIE. This place is turning into Grand Central Station in your honor.

JANET. So, would you mind if I sat in?

GRACE. No, I don't think … that is, yes, I would mind you being a fly on the wall. We've got some things to discuss privately. Society business.

JANET. Maybe we can talk later. *(Catherine enters and is horrified to see Jan.)*

GRACE. Yes. Certainly. Catherine!

CATHERINE. Dearest …

GRACE. You remember Miss Logan? From *The New York Times?*

CATHERINE. I see you made it back safely to our little town.

JANET. Montgomery is hardly a little town anymore.

CATHERINE. Sometimes it certainly feels like one. News travels so fast.

GRACE. Yes, it does. We're going to have to excuse ourselves, Miss Logan, but I'll leave you in the very capable hands of my granddaughter who is our centennial debutante. She is well-versed in the history and traditions of The Nacirema Society.

JANET. That would be great. Do you have time? *(She reaches for her purse, withdraws her ever ready reporter's notebook.)*

GRACIE. You want to talk to *me?* Now? *(Grace and Catherine exit to the library.)*

JANET. Absolutely.

GRACIE. I've got all the time in the world. Would you like some tea?

JANET. I'm more a black coffee kinda girl. Helps me keep my wits about me.

GRACIE. Two black coffees coming up. *(Gracie exits. Jan looks around, makes some notes about the room. As the lights come up full in the library, Jan stands up, looks at the portraits and makes more notes. Grace closes the library door.)*

CATHERINE. Oh, my poor darling! I forgot she was coming today. It never rains but it pours!

GRACE. Keep your voice down! She already asked if she could be a fly on the wall.

CATHERINE. What does that mean?

GRACE. It means the walls have ears.

CATHERINE. Flies on the wall, walls with ears! Is nothing sacred?

GRACE. Apparently not.

CATHERINE. Oh, Grace, how could this happen?

GRACE. How does anything happen? The point is, Lillie's daughter has a letter.

CATHERINE. Not *the* letter?

GRACE. *(She goes to the desk, opens the box, takes out the sheet of lined paper.)* I tried to tell myself that maybe he just wanted to be sure she was taken care of ...

CATHERINE. There never was any real proof, dearest. Just a crumpled draft of a note he probably never even sent.

GRACE. ... but I always knew it was more than that.

CATHERINE. Sometimes I wish I'd never found it when we cleaned out his desk.

GRACE. But you did.

CATHERINE. Yes, but it's just a few lines. How can you be sure?

GRACE. Have you forgotten the salutations he tried out? *(She reads from the paper.)* My dear Lillie. Not good enough. He crossed that out and started again. *My dear, dear Lillie.* Still not good enough. He crossed that out and tried again. *My darling Lillie ... (She stops suddenly, unable to continue.)*

CATHERINE. Don't, dearest ...

GRACE. If Dunbar wasn't already dead, I would kill him for this.

CATHERINE. What else does it say?

GRACE. Don't you remember?

CATHERINE. That was seven years ago, Grace. You can't expect

41

me to recall every last detail.

GRACE. *(Resumes reading.) In the morning, I will mail the attached letter since you have asked me not to bring it. When I'm gone, take it to Hank Graham at the law office and he'll handle everything.*

CATHERINE. Well, there you are! Did you call Hank and ask him if he ever received such a letter?

GRACE. Of course not. He would have told Doris and how long do you think it would have been before the story was all over town?

CATHERINE. Then what are you going to do?

GRACE. I'm going to pay her for the letter.

CATHERINE. Pay her? How much?

GRACE. Whatever she wants!

CATHERINE. Yes, of course. That's wise. That's very wise. *(A beat.)* How much does she want?

GRACE. She didn't say specifically. We just sort of talked around it.

CATHERINE. Well, you're going to have to offer her something specific.

GRACE. I guess you're right. But how much?

CATHERINE. A hundred dollars?

GRACE. Nobody blackmails anybody for a hundred dollars!

CATHERINE. A thousand?

GRACE. I don't have any idea. I've never been blackmailed before.

CATHERINE. Maybe she's supposed to tell you how much she wants.

GRACE. That would make sense, wouldn't it? Maybe she's going to do it on Friday when she comes for dinner.

CATHERINE. She's coming for dinner? With us?

GRACE. Marie invited her, don't ask me why, but it works to our advantage, I think. We'll be on our home turf when it's time to make our offer.

CATHERINE. Reporters, blackmailers, offers, counter offers! What's next, Grace?

GRACE. Another Dr. Dunbar, apparently. The granddaughter has been accepted at Meharry in the fall.

CATHERINE. They don't call themselves Dunbar, do they?

GRACE. No, Catherine. Not yet …

CATHERINE. Thank God! That would just be too much.

GRACE. I don't intend to mention any of this to Gracie or Marie and I will trust you not to speak to anyone about it either.

CATHERINE. My lips are sealed. *Absolutely sealed!* And once you have that letter in your hands, we'll burn it and be done with this nasty business once and for all.

GRACE. How am I going to do that?

CATHERINE. Well, I was thinking the fireplace, but ...

GRACE. No, I mean how are we going to hear her offer, give her a check and get the letter back in the middle of a dinner party?

CATHERINE. Oh, dear. I hadn't thought about that.

GRACE. I'm the hostess so everybody will be watching me ... maybe I can get her off to one side long enough to ... *(A beat.)* No. You'll have to do it.

CATHERINE. Do what?

GRACE. Be the go-between. You'll have to make her tell you what she wants and then bring me the letter so I can write her a check.

CATHERINE. What if she won't tell me?

GRACE. Why wouldn't she tell you? She's a blackmailer, isn't she?

CATHERINE. Oh, Lord, Grace! I just don't think I want to get involved.

GRACE. Are you prepared to have this kind of scandal be what takes us into our second hundred years?

CATHERINE. Of course not, but it ... it wasn't my husband, was it?

GRACE. *(A beat.)* I see. *(She turns away.)*

CATHERINE. I'm sorry, Grace. I didn't mean that.

GRACE. You don't have to apologize, Catherine. It's just that with all that talk that went on about John and Gladys Allen, I thought you might be more understanding.

CATHERINE. That was just a rumor!

GRACE. So is this as far as anyone knows! But once it hits the front page of *The New York Times,* I don't think anybody will doubt its veracity for a second. We'll be immortalized as a bunch of low-class country Negroes. I can just see the headline: *Lies and Love Child Mar Centennial Celebration.*

CATHERINE. *(A beat.)* All right. Tell me what I have to do. *(Grace and Catherine continue to talk although we no longer hear them. Lights up full in living room. Gracie returns with coffee on a silver tray. She pours gracefully like her grandmother, but is clearly eager for conversation with her idol.)*

JANET. I guess congratulations are in order.

GRACIE. For being the centennial deb? It's no big deal. I knew I

43

was going to be it. I'm the only legacy in my generation.

JANET. You lost me.

GRACIE. People who can actually trace their blood back to one of the founders are called legacies. Gram is a legacy, so my dad was, so I am. If there's a legacy girl available, she's always deb of the year. If there's a legacy guy, he escorts the girl. It's part of the tradition, but thanks anyway.

JANET. That's fascinating, but I meant congratulations on your engagement.

GRACIE. Did my grandmother tell you that?

JANET. Mrs. Green told me on the phone last week.

GRACIE. I am not engaged. Bobby Green and I grew up together and he's like a big brother to me, but since he's a legacy and we're not blood related, our grandmothers are beside themselves with plans to breed us.

JANET. Don't you want to get married?

GRACIE. I'm not interested in being anybody's wife. I'm going to be a writer.

JANET. A journalist?

GRACIE. Short stories for now. Maybe novels later.

JANET. Well good for you. The more the merrier.

GRACIE. I guess people tell you that all the time, but I'm serious. I have it all planned. I've been accepted into the Creative Writing program at Barnard. I'm going to graduate in May and move to New York.

JANET. Congratulations. Have you ever been there?

GRACIE. Once. My mother took me to see a Broadway play for my thirteenth birthday. Joseph drove us up so we didn't have to use the Jim Crow car and when we got there, we stayed at the Plaza hotel.

JANET. How'd you like it?

GRACIE. It was wonderful! It was all wonderful. We saw Central Park, the Statue of Liberty, the Bronx Zoo, the United Nations and Langston Hughes' house.

JANET. Who took you there?

GRACIE. To Mr. Hughes' house? My mother. You know how mothers read their children fairy tales at bedtime? My mother used to read me Langston Hughes stories. She loves him. So she had Joseph take us up to Harlem. I don't know how she knew where he lived, but when we got there, she got out and rang the doorbell like she'd been invited. Thank goodness he wasn't home! I don't know what she would have said if he had answered.

JANET. Who's Joseph?

GRACIE. He's Gram's chauffeur. Well, he used to work for Gram. Now he works for Mrs. Green, too, because her chauffeur retired right after Dr. Green died. They sort of share his time.

JANET. Are you sure you want to give up all this and come to New York to be a starving artist?

GRACIE. I guess some of this sounds pretty silly to you. Sometimes it seems silly to me, too, but it's kind of like growing up royal. It doesn't seem weird because everybody you know lives the same way you do, but in New York? People live all kinds of ways, not just the way it is at Plaza Hotel and that's what I want to experience. The other side of life. The side where people are struggling just to feed their families. Where every encounter can mean life or death. Real life, where love takes over everything and won't turn you loose.

JANET. *(Amused.)* Tell me about your stories. Do they have happy endings?

GRACIE. Sometimes.

JANET. Here's my one piece of advice. People love a happy ending. Give them a good package tied up with a bow and they'll buy it every time.

GRACIE. I'm not writing to sell. I'm writing to express myself.

JANET. About love?

GRACIE. Right now, yes. See, I think there's only three things worth writing about — love, honor and death. I'm going to take them in order. I've never been in love, so I'm trying to write about it dispassionately before I actually experience it and my objectivity goes out the window. *(Light up in the library. Grace puts the letter back in the box and locks it before she and Catherine come downstairs, prompting a last question from Janet.)*

JANET. How does your grandmother feel about you going to New York?

GRACIE. Oh, she doesn't know it yet. *(Suddenly concerned.)* Should I have said "off the record"?

JANET. Don't worry. I'll never tell.

GRACIE. Thanks! *(Enter Catherine and Grace from the library.)* You're too late, Gram. I told all the family secrets.

GRACE. We have no family secrets.

CATHERINE. Goodbye all! *(She exits.)*

GRACE. Will you excuse us, dear? Miss Logan and I have a little business to attend to.

GRACIE. Yes, ma'am. I enjoyed talking with you.

JANET. Me, too. I'd love to see one of your stories some time.

GRACIE. For real?

GRACE. Don't say *for real*, dear. Say *really?*

JANET. Pick the best one and I'll give it a read.

GRACIE. Thank you! Thank you so much!

GRACE. Don't forget to change for dinner.

GRACIE. Yes, ma'am. *(Gracie exits upstairs. Grace turns to Jan and smiles hospitably.)*

JANET. Alone at last.

GRACE. Would you care to join me in a glass of sherry?

JANET. Thank you. *(Grace pours the sherry, offers one to Janet.)*

GRACE. May I clear the air?

JANET. By all means.

GRACE. The reason I didn't return your calls the last time you were here was not just because of our first unfortunate exchange, but because my granddaughter had been reading your stories to me for several months and frankly I didn't see anything there that indicated to me you would have an appreciation of an organization like ours.

JANET. I'm sorry you felt that way.

GRACE. It is my hope that once you've had a chance to get to know us a little better, you'll see that we play a valuable role in the Negro community and your next story will reflect that.

JANET. I understand that the commemorative bust of Dr. Dunbar is going to cost almost two thousand dollars. *(Grace is surprised but recovers quickly.)*

GRACE. We believe in doing everything first class at Nacirema.

JANET. Was there ever any thought of using some of that money for scholarships or will that come later?

GRACE. Let me try to explain something to you. The Nacirema Society is not a social service group nor a political organization. Our challenge and our joy is to celebrate the best of us, not by giving scholarships and financial assistance, but by recognizing the fact that there are some of us who don't need it. *(A beat.)* Who have never needed it.

JANET. I see.

GRACE. I don't think you do. My great grandmother used to say

46

there are black folks and white folks and then there's us, the best of both worlds. I used to think she meant because of the unfortunate racial mixture that occurred in our family while we were being held in bondage, but now I know that she wasn't talking about color at all. She was talking about class, culture, education, refinement. Those Nacirema white dresses were our suits of armor, our protection from who they said we were and our assertion of who we know ourselves to be. So this cotillion, this one hundredth anniversary celebration, is more than some little brown girls, waltzing around in poofy white dresses. It is a way of claiming our rightful place in the world and holding it fast for those whose lives may not yet permit such refinements, but one day will. *(A beat. She puts down her glass and stands up.)* Well, it's getting late. We'll barely have time to dress for dinner.

JANET. Mrs. Dunbar. *(Grace turns.)* I'm afraid this is about as dressed as I get.

GRACE. Oh. What were you planning to wear to the ball?

JANET. I brought an evening skirt.

GRACE. Well, this is evening, so that will be fine. Was there anything else?

JANET. I just want you to know that I'm here as a reporter. I'm going to do my best to blend in, as your houseguest, but you do understand that I'm always working.

GRACE. I completely understand.

JANET. Sometimes people get confused.

GRACE. *(Smiles.)* I never get confused. Dinner in half an hour. Don't be late. *(Black.)*

Scene 6

Lights up on the kitchen. Lillie is still sitting at the table with a now cold cup of coffee. Her backpack is still where she dropped it when she arrived. She is studying the clipping, now badly crumpled but still spread on the table before her.

The door opens to admit Alpha. She is highly agitated after her meeting with Grace but cautiously optimistic that things went well. She is trying to figure out where she's going to get the letter she promised to produce since, in reality, she has no such letter in her possession. So preoccupied is she that when she enters, she has almost forgotten about Lillie.

ALPHA. Good Lord, girl! You scared me half to death! I thought you'd be upstairs in the middle of a nice long nap by now.
LILLIE. I never take naps.
ALPHA. Well, you're a big girl. Naps are not required. *(Taking off her coat, hat, etc.)* You hungry? Thelma starts serving dinner at five.
LILLIE. *(Holds up the clipping.)* Do you know these people?
ALPHA. Those aren't people. Those are Dunbars.
LILLIE. He's not a Dunbar.
ALPHA. *(She looks at the photo with contempt.)* The thing is, it wasn't Dr. Dunbar. He was a pretty good guy. It was Grace. She was always so snooty. Even today, when I said … *(Stops on a dime when she realizes she's about to tell too much, too soon.)*
LILLIE. You saw Mrs. Dunbar today?
ALPHA. *(She takes the clipping and tacks it back on the bulletin board.)* I … I just bumped into her at the lawyer's office. We got to talking for a minute. That's her granddaughter next to the Green kid. They're only allowed to marry each other. *(She suddenly frowns at the crumpled paper.)* Who crumpled it up like this?
LILLIE. I did.
ALPHA. Not crazy about the Dunbars either, huh?
LILLIE. That's my friend.
ALPHA. Who? Her?

LILLIE. No. *Him.*

ALPHA. You know this fool?

LILLIE. He's not a fool!

ALPHA. Okay, he's the King of England. Did you all meet over tea and crumpets at Buckingham Palace?

LILLIE. No. Biology.

ALPHA. *(Suddenly dawning.)* When you say your friend, do you mean Prince Charming? *(Lillie nods miserably.)*

ALPHA. The fool who's sending you back to the wilds of Mississippi all by yourself?

LILLIE. He's not a fool!

ALPHA. What are you really doing here?

LILLIE. *(A beat.)* I came to talk to Bobby.

ALPHA. About what? His engagement?

LILLIE. It's a mistake! They just got things mixed up. That's an old picture. See, it says right there. December, 1963. That's way last year!

ALPHA. Did he ever tell you anything about little Miss Gracie Dunbar?

LILLIE. He told me he loved me, but he didn't deserve me.

ALPHA. Well, at least me and the Prince agree on that. Has he told his family about you?

LILLIE. No … but I hadn't told you about him either.

ALPHA. But that was because you know I have good reason to dislike that crowd, with their secret societies and their chauffeured limousines.

LILLIE. They probably have their reasons for not liking us, too.

ALPHA. No, they don't. They just think they're better than we are because they've been reading longer, but none of that matters. He showed you his true colors. Take him at his word and good riddance!

LILLIE. *(Takes her mother's hand.)* Place your hand against my heart and say his name. *(She begins to cry.)*

ALPHA. I'm sorry, baby. Don't cry. Here, blow your nose. *(Lillie does. Loudly.)*

ALPHA. Better?

LILLIE. I came here to make him tell me to my face.

ALPHA. Oh, sweetie. That never works like you think it will. Trust me.

LILLIE. I don't know what's going on with that girl in the picture or whatever would make him say the things he said, but I think if I can find him, if we can talk face to face, I'll know the truth.

ALPHA. The truth about what?

LILLIE. About everything.

ALPHA. That's a pretty tall order.

LILLIE. Isn't that what you always say? The truth, the whole truth and nothing but the truth.

ALPHA. *(Suddenly guilty at the secret between them.)* Yes. That's what I always say.

LILLIE. What's wrong?

ALPHA. I figured out a way to raise your tuition for Meharry.

LILLIE. Stop worrying about that. I've applied for another loan. I'll get a part-time job.

ALPHA. You shouldn't have to get a job! You got a full scholarship from Fisk and you deserve the same from Meharry. If you were a boy graduating at the top of your class, you can bet you'd have a free ride.

LILLIE. *(A beat.)* We've been over and over all this. Why are you bringing it up now?

ALPHA. *(A beat. She decides to come clean.)* Okay. Here's the thing. I didn't just bump into Grace Dunbar at the lawyer's office today. I went to her house.

LILLIE. I thought you hated her.

ALPHA. *(Laughs a little.)* I swear, it's going to sound crazy to you when I say it out loud, but don't jump to any conclusions until you hear me out. Just remember all the years Mama worked over there for that little piece of change Grace Dunbar paid her. Don't ever forget that.

LILLIE. You didn't go over there and demand reparations, did you?

ALPHA. *(Startled at how close Lillie came to the truth.)* Not exactly. I just told her that I was Dr. Dunbar's outside child and if she didn't play along, I'd be forced to go down to *The Advertiser* and spill the beans just in time for her big centennial moment.

LILLIE. *(Beyond shocked.)* You what?

ALPHA. See? *(The nervous laugh again.)* I told you it might sound a little crazy at first.

LILLIE. You told her that Grandmom and Dr. Dunbar had a child? And it was *you?*

ALPHA. It was nothing she hadn't heard before. That was a big rumor around here, once upon a time. When I was a kid, people used to tease me about it. One day, it upset me so much I ran home crying and told mama, and you know what she said? She said it wasn't true, but if it was, I could do a lot worse for a daddy than Louis Dunbar.

LILLIE. But she said it wasn't true!

ALPHA. Listen, more than anything, Mama wanted you to be a doctor. She dreamed that dream at least as hard as you did. If tossing this tall tale around one last time will help make it real, I think she'd say *more power to us!*

LILLIE. So what does all this have to do with my tuition? *(Alpha is silent. A beat. It dawns on Lillie.)* Oh, no! Please tell me you didn't try to extort money from Grace Dunbar with this crazy story!

ALPHA. She's the one who brought up money. Not me.

LILLIE. What makes you think she won't call the police?

ALPHA. And tell them what? That her former maid's only daughter is also her late husband's outside child? That's not a crime, darling. That's a scandal and these people hate scandal like cats hate cold water. She'll be happy to pay whatever we ask if we promise to go back where we came from and leave them to do whatever Dunbars do when nobody's around to keep an eye on things.

LILLIE. Mom! Don't do this! We'll figure something out. I promise!

ALPHA. I have figured something out. If you hadn't come down here, mooning over *young master Green,* the next sound you would have heard would be the sound of your tuition being paid in full for the next four years. It's only fair.

LILLIE. If it's only fair, why don't we just ask her for the money?

ALPHA. Like a handout? I wouldn't give Grace Dunbar the satisfaction!

LILLIE. You'd rather blackmail her?

ALPHA. Blackmail is an ugly word. This is a simple business transaction between two grown women.

LILLIE. I'll tell them it isn't true.

ALPHA. That's works to my advantage. Shows I never told a soul, even you, his granddaughter. Proves I can be discreet.

LILLIE. A useful trait in a blackmailer.

ALPHA. There is one more thing.

LILLIE. *(Groans.)* You didn't stop and rob a bank on the way home, did you?

ALPHA. No, but I did tell Grace Dunbar a little white lie.

LILLIE. In addition to the big black one?

ALPHA. Don't be fresh. I told her I had a letter from Dr. Dunbar to your grandmother admitting paternity. So Grace said she was sorry for doubting me and that I should bring the letter to dinner on Friday. We're both invited to this shindig, by the way. You'll need something to wear. These people dress for dinner.

LILLIE. But there is no letter.

ALPHA. There will be by Friday. I'm going to write one. Nothing fancy. Short and sweet, just like I told her today.

LILLIE. Don't you think they'll recognize his handwriting?

ALPHA. That's why I'm going to take it over to the Baptist church. They've got the oldest typewriters in the world.

LILLIE. This will never work.

ALPHA. Of course it will. You probably need some shoes, too.

LILLIE. I'm not going over there for dinner!

ALPHA. Aren't you even a little bit curious to see your rival up close?

LILLIE. What rival? *(Alpha points at the clipping.)*

ALPHA. That one. I happen to know she'll be there. You come with me. After I get the check, you can give her a piece of your mind and we'll blow this town!

LILLIE. You don't think he'll be there, do you?

ALPHA. I don't think so. From what I heard, it's ladies night.

LILLIE. Is there any way I can talk you out of this?

ALPHA. Is there any way I can talk you out of going to Greenwood?

LILLIE. It's not the same thing!

ALPHA. Okay, well here's an idea. How about after we finish up with our rich relations, *I* come with you to Mississippi?

LILLIE. Don't try to change the subject.

ALPHA. I'm serious.

LILLIE. What are you going to do? Teach them how to con people out of money?

ALPHA. I don't have to teach anybody anything. Don't you need people to roll bandages and stuff?

LILLIE. This isn't the Civil War. The bandages are already rolled.

ALPHA. How about typing?

LILLIE. They don't have a typewriter.

ALPHA. You mean to tell me there's not one thing those Mississippi Negroes need that I can provide?

LILLIE. Just one. *Me.*

ALPHA. How'd you get to be so hard headed?

LILLIE. It's in the blood!
ALPHA. Probably on the Dunbar side. *(Black.)*

Scene 7

Lights up on Gracie in the library. It is 3 A.M. and the house is quiet except for the clicking of Gracie's typewriter. She types, reads, makes corrections, types. She is totally engrossed in her work. She is wearing pajamas, bathrobe and pink fuzzy slippers. The sound of pebbles against the library window brings her back to the world with a start. She listens. More pebbles. This is a sound with which she is familiar. She gets up quickly, pulling her bathrobe around her a little tighter, and goes to the window. She looks out, waves and points a signal to the person she recognizes outside the window.

Heading quickly downstairs, Gracie moves through the darkened house to the front door. She opens it to admit Bobby Green. Motioning for him to be quiet and to follow her, she leads him upstairs to the library, a room he knows well. A beat too late, Jessie appears at the door to admit the guest. She is wearing a robe, house slippers, a night cap over rollers. She opens the door, looks, finds no one there, closes it and exits back to bed.

GRACIE. Are you drunk?
BOBBY. Not even a little bit. What are you doing up so late?
GRACIE. I'm training myself to write between three and seven. That way, if I have to get a nine-to-five job, I'll be able to get in four hours of writing time before I have to go to work. What are *you* doing up so early?
BOBBY. Contemplating the fact that I'm a complete idiot.
GRACIE. So what else is new? Want some coffee?
BOBBY. No. I need some advice.
GRACIE. From me? About what?
BOBBY. What are you always talking about? What are you always

writing about? Love, right? So here's the question ... do you believe in it?

GRACIE. As much as I believe the sun is going to rise in the east and set in the west. It's practically all I do believe in unequivocally.

BOBBY. Would you risk everything on account of it?

GRACIE. It's not a real love story if you don't risk everything.

BOBBY. Even ... money?

GRACIE. *Especially* money!

BOBBY. All right. That settles it then. Gracie, I can't escort you to the ball on Saturday.

GRACIE. Yeah, right. Our grandmothers would compete for the right to kill you.

BOBBY. I've got a friend from school lined up for you. He can wear my tails and both his grandfathers are in The Boule, so he can waltz his ass off.

GRACIE. You're not kidding, are you?

BOBBY. Last summer, I got to know a woman who brought out the best in me. A woman who makes me think better and laugh louder. *(A beat. He can't believe these feelings himself.)* When I'm not with her, I feel like one of my arms is missing.

GRACIE. Oh, Bobby, you're in love!

BOBBY. That's what I've been trying to tell you, kid. I've got it bad.

GRACIE. That's so romantic! Go on!

BOBBY. I promised her I'd spend Christmas break in Mississippi volunteering at this clinic with her. We've been talking about it for weeks. I forgot all about the Centennial Ball.

GRACIE. *(Teasing.)* How could you be expected to remember? It only comes around once every hundred years.

BOBBY. But when I told my grandmother I was going to Mississippi, she read me the riot act. She said if I didn't cancel my plans, she would write me out of her will once and for all.

GRACIE. She would never do that.

BOBBY. Yes. She would. *(A beat.)* So, I called my friend and told her I couldn't go with her, that I wasn't the man she thought I was even though that's the man I want to be, and I hung up.

GRACIE. You hung up on the woman you love?

BOBBY. I told you I was an idiot. I'm going to make a few mistakes.

GRACIE. So what are you going to do about it?

BOBBY. I've been driving around all night, trying to decide. First, I'd try to think about all that money, but I kept getting distracted thinking about the way this girl laughs. Then I tried thinking about losing all that money and I kept remembering the way she smells, so I tried thinking about what my life would be like without all that money and all I could think about was what my life would be like without her in it. *(A beat.)* So I'm going to write my grandmother a letter telling her to keep her money because not being with the woman I love for five minutes is worse than being poor every day for the rest of my life. And then I'm going to Mississippi and tell this amazing woman that I've been the biggest fool god ever made for even *thinking* I could live without her. *(He's realizing this as he says it out loud.)* And then I'm going to get down on one knee and I'm going to beg her forgiveness as if I was all five of the Temptations rolled into one and then I'm going to ask her if she will do me the great honor of becoming my wife. *(A beat.)*

GRACIE. *Wow!*

BOBBY. So what do you think?

GRACIE. It's wonderful, but as love stories go, you've still got one big problem.

BOBBY. You don't think she'll forgive me?

GRACIE. *She'll* be the least of it. *I'll* never forgive you if you just leave a note for your grandmother and slink off into the night.

BOBBY. I hadn't exactly settled on slinking. I was just hoping to avoid another confrontation.

GRACIE. You said you wanted to risk everything. Well if you're serious then you have to stand up to your grandmother once and for all and tell her being rich doesn't give her the right to run other people's lives.

BOBBY. Listen, kid, this isn't one of your stories where the knight rides up to the castle and slays the dragon.

GRACIE. Why isn't it?

BOBBY. Because this is my real life, remember?

GRACIE. Well, in case you change your mind, I understand you and the dragon in question are invited to dinner with us on Friday. That might be a good time. All concerned parties will be present, except your true love, who will have to hear the story later to understand your courage under grandmotherly fire.

BOBBY. You want me to make a general announcement?

GRACIE. Of course I do. If you don't, you leave me trying to explain, and you know I always embellish!

BOBBY. *(A beat.)* And if I slay the dragon, speak my speech, and stride off to claim my beloved, can you promise me a happy ending?

GRACIE. I can absolutely guarantee it!

BOBBY. All right then. You've got a deal! *(They hug.)*

GRACIE. Now get out of here, so I can get back to work.

BOBBY. I'll take the window for old time's sake.

GRACIE. I'm proud of you, Dr. Green. I always knew there was more to you than meets the eye.

BOBBY. *(Turns to exit the window.)* Here's looking at you, kid!

GRACIE. *Bobby!*

BOBBY. What?

GRACIE. You didn't tell me her name!

BOBBY. Lillie! Her name is Lillie! *(Bobby exits. Gracie goes back to her typewriter.)*

End of Act One

ACT TWO

Scene 1

Lights up on Gracie. She is alone in the living room. Motown music is blasting from the stereo: an upbeat R&B song appropriate to the time period plays. She is singing along, she may dance a little. She has notes, some books, etc., laid out on the coffee table and the couch. She's working on her senior project. The music is so loud she doesn't hear the doorbell. Jesse goes to the door, admits Lillie, who enters the living room. She stands for a minute until Gracie sees her and goes immediately to turn the music down.

GRACIE. I'm so sorry! I thought Jessie and I had the house to ourselves. I'm Gracie Dunbar. Are you here to see my mom?

LILLIE. *(Startled.)* You're Gracie Dunbar?

GRACIE. Yes. Have we met?

LILLIE. I saw your picture in the paper.

GRACIE. I hope you won't hold that against me.

LILLIE. I'm Alpha's daughter.

GRACIE. The one who is going to Meharry?

LILLIE. How do you know that?

GRACIE. *(She picks up her school materials.)* Your mother was over here bragging about you. Congratulations! I was looking forward to meeting you at dinner on Friday and here you are. Come on in.

LILLIE. *(Hesitates.)* Is your grandmother at home?

GRACIE. I'm sorry, she's not. It's going to be pretty hard to catch her around here until after the cotillion, but you'll meet her at dinner. Even Gram has to sit down to eat.

LILLIE. That's what I wanted to talk to her about. *Friday.*

GRACIE. You're still coming, aren't you? I know Gram is looking forward to meeting you and there's going to be a reporter here from *The New York Times.*

LILLIE. I don't think so.

GRACIE. Why not? You're more than welcome. We all loved your grandmother very much.

LILLIE. Good. That's why you should know there is absolutely no truth to the whole dad thing. *(Her words rush out before she can stop them.)*

GRACIE. What dad thing?

LILLIE. My mom had a bout of temporary insanity where she thought blackmail would be the best way for her to raise some money, but she was wrong. So we won't be coming to dinner, but we won't be going to the papers either, so tell your grandmother there is no need to involve the police.

GRACIE. *(Totally confused.)* My dad died when I was seven.

LILLIE. I'm not talking about your dad. I'm talking about …

GRACIE. I don't think I ever met your dad.

LILLIE. You really don't know what I'm talking about, do you?

GRACIE. No, but I'd like to.

LILLIE. My mom is threatening to resurrect a rumor that your grandfather is … my grandfather, too.

GRACIE. My granddaddy Dunbar?

LILLIE. That's the one.

GRACIE. And Lillie?

LILLIE. My grandmother.

GRACIE. Wow …

LILLIE. Is that so hard to believe?

GRACIE. No … yes … I mean, you never really think about your grandfather having sex with anybody but your grandmother — and I don't even like to think too much about that! — but this is — do you think it's true?

LILLIE. My mother knows how much your family hates scandal, so she picked the most scandalous thing she could think of.

GRACIE. So your mom knows it's not true and she's prepared to risk everything anyway?

LILLIE. She's an attempted blackmailer. Truth is beside the point. I just want your grandmother to know any arrangement she had with my mother is off.

GRACIE. What's the money for?

LILLIE. Does it matter?

GRACIE. It does to me. I'm a writer. Motivation is everything.

LILLIE. Just tell your grandmother what I said. We don't want any trouble.

GRACIE. Does your mom have a criminal record?

LILLIE. Of course not.

GRACIE. Ever been arrested?

LILLIE. Never!

GRACIE. *(A beat.)* It's for tuition, isn't it?

LILLIE. That's none of your business.

GRACIE. Your mom exhibited uncharacteristic and extreme behavior in order to address a crisis — the crushing of her only daughter's dream. Her love for you made it worth the risk.

LILLIE. Did she tell you all that?

GRACIE. No. I made it up from what you just said. *(Grinning at her own imagination.)* Pretty close though, huh?

LILLIE. You think this is funny?

GRACIE. No. I just meant that, as a writing exercise, it makes a great story.

LILLIE. A writing exercise? My mother is right. Everything is a game to you people. I don't know why I ever thought he was any different.

GRACIE. My granddaddy?

LILLIE. Your fiancé. I hope the two of you will be very happy together.

GRACIE. What fiancé?

LILLIE. I saw his picture in the paper with you.

GRACIE. That's not my fiancé. That's just Bobby Green. We grew up together. Our grandmothers think it's our destiny to marry each other and carry on the line for another hundred years. They're convinced if they say it loud enough we'll think it's our idea.

LILLIE. Then you're not really engaged to … that guy?

GRACIE. No way!

LILLIE. You're not … going to marry him?

GRACIE. He's like my big brother. I've never even kissed him on the lips. *(Lillie bursts into tears.)*

LILLIE. I knew it couldn't be true. I knew he would have told me.

GRACIE. Told you what?

LILLIE. About you!

GRACIE. What about me?

LILLIE. That he was in love with you.

GRACIE. Bobby isn't in love with me. He's madly in love with a girl who … *(She realizes who it is.)* Are you … *Bobby's Lillie?*

LILLIE. I thought I was.

GRACIE. You were! You are! You are! You're Lillie! He's going to Mississippi to find you right after dinner tomorrow night!

LILLIE. But what about his grandmother? She's going to disinherit him or something.

GRACIE. He doesn't care about any of that. He said without you, his life wasn't worth living.

LILLIE. Bobby said that?

GRACIE. His exact words were — *(She flips to a page in her notebook.)* "Not being with the woman I love for five minutes is worse than being poor every day for the rest of my life."

LILLIE. You wrote it down?

GRACIE. I write everything down. So what are you going to do?

LILLIE. I guess I'll go on to Mississippi and pretend to be surprised when he gets there.

GRACIE. If you want to surprise him, we can do better than that.

LILLIE. What do you mean?

GRACIE. He's going to tell his grandmother everything at dinner on Friday.

LILLIE. In front of everybody?

GRACIE. Well, he is the King of the Centennial Cotillion of The Nacirema Society of Montgomery, Alabama and the escort to yours truly, Queen Gracie Dunbar so he can't exactly slip out of town unnoticed.

LILLIE. I guess you're right.

GRACIE. So he's going to wait until everybody arrives for dinner and then he's going to tell them he has decided that nothing is more important to him than the woman he loves and that he can't be at the ball because he's leaving right that very minute to be at your side as you do the necessary and dangerous work that is required to build a new and better world.

LILLIE. *(A beat.)* I'd love to read one of your stories.

GRACIE. Wait! Here's where the surprise comes in. As he kisses his grandmother's cheek to show there's no hard feelings, and turns to go, you will step out suddenly from where you have been standing, just out of sight *here. (She indicates the stairs to the library.)* And walk into his open arms. After that, you have to improvise!

LILLIE. You make it sound like a fairy tale.

GRACIE. It is a fairy tale. Love conquers all!

LILLIE. Do you really believe that?

GRACIE. Of course! And so do you or you wouldn't have gone

to Mississippi in the first place and Bobby never would have come to protect you and fallen in love so hard he finally figured out that working for a living isn't the worst thing that can happen to a full-grown man.

LILLIE. *(Grins at Gracie.)* Or a full grown woman.

GRACIE. Does your mother know you came here?

LILLIE. No. She's over at the Baptist Church working on the fake letter.

GRACIE. What fake letter?

LILLIE. Your grandmother demanded proof or she'd call the sheriff, so my mom said she had a letter from Dr. Dunbar admitting everything. She's supposed to bring it on Friday so they can make the switch. She's typing it up at the church because they have real old typewriters.

GRACIE. Your mother's good at this.

LILLIE. That's what she keeps telling me.

GRACIE. Well, don't tell her that we talked. Just tell her you changed your mind about the dinner and if you can't talk her out of it, you're not prepared to let her come alone.

LILLIE. What good will that do?

GRACIE. Once everybody gets here, just leave everything to me.

LILLIE. Are you sure?

GRACIE. Are you?

LILLIE. Absolutely.

GRACIE. You know, I'm almost sorry there's no truth to that rumor.

LILLIE. Why? Because then my mom wouldn't be trying to blackmail your grandmother?

GRACIE. No, because then we'd be cousins.

LILLIE. See you Friday.

GRACIE. Don't be late.

LILLIE. Not a chance! *(Lillie exits. Jessie opens the door. Gracie turns the music back up loud: a song like "Baby Love" by the Supremes.* She begins to gather up her things as we go to black.)*

---

* See Special Note on Songs and Recordings on copyright page.

Scene 2

Catherine is in the living room, pacing. Jessie appears at the front door. Grace enters, gives Jessie her coat and sweeps into the living area. She is surprised to see Catherine.

GRACE. To what do I owe this pleasant surprise?
CATHERINE. Oh, my God! I thought you'd never get here.
GRACE. Well, here I am.
CATHERINE. I just don't think I can go through with it, Grace. I really don't!
GRACE. Of course you can. We've already agreed.
CATHERINE. But what if I say something wrong?
GRACE. All you have to do is get the letter and tell her I need a dollar figure to put on the check and she'll give you one.
CATHERINE. What if it's too much?
GRACE. Then I'll tell you and you'll tell her.
CATHERINE. *(Groans.)* See? That's what I'm afraid of. Back and forth, carrying messages. I'll be a regular Mata Hari and you know what happened to her!
GRACE. No, actually I don't.
CATHERINE. Well, I don't either, but it was something unpleasant, I'm sure of that, but that's not the point. I just don't know why *I* have to be the go-between. You know when I get nervous it's hard for me to stick to a plan. I get confused!
GRACE. You won't get confused.
CATHERINE. You said that when we had that dinner party for those African diplomats and you see what happened.
GRACE. That's because they were speaking French!
CATHERINE. All I'm saying is, this is a dangerous game we're playing, Grace Dunbar, and it's got to go off without a hitch. Even while we're engaged in these nefarious activities, we must appear to be as above reproach as Lot's wife.
GRACE. As Calpurnia.
CATHERINE. What?
GRACE. Lot's wife turned into a pillar of salt. Ceasar's wife was

above reproach. *Calpurnia.* That was her name.

CATHERINE. *(Wailing.)* You see? I'm already confused!

GRACE. All right. Just calm down. I'll tell Marie.

CATHERINE. You will?

GRACE. That way if you get turned around, there will be some-one else there who knows the plan.

CATHERINE. I feel better already. Thank you, dearest.

GRACE. You're going to be fine. Our foremothers held off slave owners, rebel soldiers, carpetbaggers and the Ku Klux Klan. I be-lieve we can handle one amateur blackmailer from Harlem!

CATHERINE. You're right!

GRACE. Of course I'm right. Just be your usual gracious and charming self and by the end of the evening, this will all just be an unpleasant memory.

CATHERINE. Like okra on a holiday table! *(Enter Marie from upstairs.)*

MARIE. You're not changing the menu again are you?

CATHERINE. *(Jumps guiltily.)* Oh, Marie! You startled me!

GRACE. Catherine was just being a worry wart.

CATHERINE. Guilty as charged, but I feel a lot better now. Where's that beautiful daughter of yours?

MARIE. She's out with our houseguest, showing her the neighbor-hood.

CATHERINE. Do you think that's wise?

GRACE. Of course it is. You couldn't ask for a better goodwill ambassador.

MARIE. Gracie is a big fan.

CATHERINE. I hope Miss Logan doesn't tell her what I said about the engagement.

GRACE and MARIE. What did you say?

CATHERINE. That there definitely was one?

MARIE. *(Laughs.)* Miss Catherine, you are incorrigible!

CATHERINE. I would think you'd be more cooperative on this, Marie, really. Don't you want your daughter's announcement to make *The New York Times.*

MARIE. I want her to be happy.

CATHERINE. Well, I don't know who could make her happier than my Bobby. They're perfect for each other.

GRACE. And if we just give them a minute or two, they'll prob-ably realize it without any help from us at all.

CATHERINE. You're right, you're right. I'm just a little keyed up with all that's going on. I'm running around like a chicken with my head cut off.

GRACE. That's why I'm going to give you an order as your doyenne.

CATHERINE. Order away!

GRACE. Go home. Have a glass of sherry in front of the fire and just think about how beautiful our ball will be this year.

CATHERINE. That sounds like heaven! Oh! I almost forgot! Jennie finally finished the girls' dresses!

GRACE. Where do you think I've been all afternoon?

CATHERINE. *(Laughs.)* You always take care of things, don't you?

GRACE. I do the best I can. *(Kisses Catherine's cheek.)* Now go on! Joseph hasn't even put the car in the garage yet.

CATHERINE. I don't know what I'd do without him! Or you. See you tomorrow night. *(She exits. Marie and Grace are alone.)*

GRACE. If Gracie and Bobby were madly in love, I think Catherine would manage to talk them out of it with her meddling!

MARIE. If they were madly in love, no one could talk them out of it.

GRACE. Spare me! You are the reason Gracie has those absurd romantic ideas in the first place.

MARIE. Guilty as charged. I'll have to count on you for the more practical matters.

GRACE. *(Suddenly serious.)* Marie, I have to tell you something and I don't want to have to repeat myself. It is hard enough to say this at all, but twice in a row would be unendurable, so please pay attention.

MARIE. I'm all ears.

GRACE. Sit down here by me. *(Marie does. Grace takes her hands.)* Sometimes the private lives of even those closest to us are not what they seem.

MARIE. What do you mean?

GRACE. It's so hard for me to tell you this, but many years ago, John Green fathered a child outside of his marriage to Catherine.

MARIE. *(Shocked.)* Dr. Green?!

GRACE. There had been rumors, of course, but no child had ever surfaced … until now.

MARIE. Oh, my God! How awful!

GRACE. She has come to Montgomery to threaten public exposure of the whole sordid story unless Catherine will pay the price she's asking.

MARIE. That's blackmail! Did you tell her to call the sheriff?

GRACE. She's afraid to risk telling anyone. She'd rather just pay the woman and make her disappear.

MARIE. How old is she?

GRACE. Catherine? Five years older than I am, but she'll probably say two.

MARIE. No, the child.

GRACE. She's not a child anymore. She's forty if she's a day.

MARIE. You saw her?

GRACE. So did you. She was here Tuesday.

MARIE. There was no one here Tuesday except Alpha Campbell Jackson ... *(Realizes what this means.) Lillie Campbell and Dr. Green?* I can't believe it! We talked for a good half hour before you got here and she never said a word! She was cool as a cucumber.

GRACE. Blackmailers have to be cool so they don't draw attention to themselves.

MARIE. Why did she come here instead of going to the Greens?

GRACE. She thought I would be able to facilitate matters. She knows Catherine is like a sister to me.

MARIE. The scandal would kill her if it ever got out.

GRACE. That's why we can't let that happen.

MARIE. What did she say when you told her?

GRACE. *(Question caught her by surprise.)* She ... she wept.

MARIE. Poor thing. No wonder she was a bit scattered. *(A beat.)* Don't worry. I'll keep an eye on her tomorrow night. If she needs anything, I'll be right there.

GRACE. Bless you, dear. *(Starts to exit upstairs.)* And Marie? Don't let on to Catherine that I told you any of this. She made me promise.

MARIE. Do you think she knew?

GRACE. We all knew, but our generation was raised to look the other way if that's what it took to keep the family together.

MARIE. I don't know if I could do that.

GRACE. I'm glad you never had to. *(A beat.)* Tell Jessie we'll be four for supper, will you? *(Grace exits upstairs. Black.)*

Scene 3

Lights up on Lillie at the kitchen table. She is reading the newspaper. Enter Alpha with a few shopping bags.

ALPHA. Hey, you! *(Kisses her and drops into a chair. She may kick off her high heels and wiggle her toes.)*

LILLIE. Guess what?

ALPHA. I'm too tired to guess.

LILLIE. Dr. King accepted the Nobel Peace Prize today.

ALPHA. *(Distracted.)* In Montgomery?

LILLIE. In Norway! He's the youngest person ever to get it.

ALPHA. Let me see the picture. I know he was clean.

LILLIE. No picture. This is Alabama, remember? They barely ran the story at all. Look how tiny it is. *(She pushes the paper over for Alpha to see.)*

ALPHA. *(Affectionately to Dr. King's photograph.)* Well, go ahead, Rev! Change the world with your bad self!

LILLIE. Speaking of changing the world, how's everything in the blackmailing business?

ALPHA. The way those biddies in the pastor's office were breathing down my neck, it's a wonder I could even concentrate, but it was all worth it. I now have a letter to present to Grace Dunbar that has been so perfectly produced on the oldest working Underwood manual typewriter in North America, and I use the term *working* lightly, that if she had doubts before, this letter will banish them from her mind. It is, if I do say so myself, a work of art. Wanna see it?

LILLIE. No, thanks. That would make me an accessory. What's in the bags?

ALPHA. Have you ever heard the old saying that in order to make money, you have to look like you don't need it?

LILLIE. Is that how you and your blackmailer friends talk when you get together?

ALPHA. The truth is, I was sort of hoping you might have changed your mind about not going to the dinner, and I don't want you to be sitting there like anybody's country cousin so … I bought you this!

(She pulls out a lovely, simple, elegant gown. Lillie looks at the dress. She may touch it admiringly.)

LILLIE. I can't let you do this.

ALPHA. It's done.

LILLIE. I mean, I can't let you do this *alone*.

ALPHA. You're coming with me?

LILLIE. I want you to have a witness when they carry you off to the city jail.

ALPHA. Oh, sweetie! *(Hugs her.)* I know you don't think this is a great idea, but having you there means so much to me.

LILLIE. Should I make picket signs that say *Free Alpha Campbell Jackson* and march around outside?

ALPHA. Just make sure you let me get my hair together before the press arrives. I hate those pictures where some poor woman just got arrested for sitting in somewhere and her hair is all over her head.

LILLIE. People don't care about hair in the middle of a revolution!

ALPHA. Well, maybe they should. What made you change your mind about coming?

LILLIE. *(Grins at her mother.)* The dress.

ALPHA. Then try it on. I'm dying to see if it fits. *(Lillie gets up to go change. She picks up the dress carefully.)*

LILLIE. I hope you got the shoes, too. *(Alpha reaches into another bag and hands her a shoe box.)*

LILLIE. Of course you did. *(Takes the shoe box.)*

ALPHA. Lillie?

LILLIE. Yeah?

ALPHA. Nothing bad is going to happen.

LILLIE. Can I get that in writing?

ALPHA. No problem. As long as you don't ask me to type you up a copy, I'm good to go. *(She sits, writes it out and signs it.)* Nothing … bad … is … going … to … happen. Signed, Alpha Campbell Jackson. *(She hands it to Lillie.)* There. Now you can relax!

LILLIE. I'll hold you to it.

ALPHA. Now can we do something about that hair? *(Lillie laughs and exits upstairs. Black.)*

Scene 4

Lights up full on the living room, half in the library. During this scene, there will be five main playing areas; the library, the stairs up to the library; the far end of the couch in the living room; the bar/food area; the stairs to the second floor. Since there will be several conversations going on at once, it should be established immediately that it is possible to confide in someone at the far end of the couch and not be overheard by someone else at the bar, etc.

In the library, we can see Gracie curled up on the sofa, oblivious to her beautiful gown, scribbling in her notebook. She will often pause, consider, gaze out the window, etc., before resuming her work. Downstairs, Grace, also in a beautiful gown, is moving around in the living room, checking every detail. Of course, everything is perfect.

Grace gives intimate formal dinner parties frequently and this one would be no different except for the presence of the blackmailer. An almost imperceptible unease lies beneath her perfectly poised exterior.

Enter Jan from upstairs. She is wearing her evening skirt with a black turtleneck sweater.

GRACE. Good evening.

JANET. Mrs. Dunbar, everything looks lovely.

GRACE. As do you, Miss Logan. And you were worried about having something appropriate to wear!

JANET. My friends tell me I don't have much fashion sense, but I clean up really well.

GRACE. Yes … well … sherry?

JANET. Thank you. *(She follows Grace to the bar area where Grace pours two.)* I had a great time with your granddaughter yesterday afternoon.

GRACE. I understand you dropped in on Jennie Turner.

JANET. If Gracie hadn't vouched for me, I doubt I'd be here to tell the tale.

GRACE. She's been working so hard to get everything ready for tomorrow night. It really is quite amazing to realize these same six gowns debuted in 1914 well before these girls were even a gleam in their father's eyes.

JANET. Mrs. Turner said your mother helped her quite a bit with the design.

GRACE. She's being generous. My mother took her to New York for a few days so we could get some idea of what was current up there, but the design was all Jennie. She's a genius.

JANET. Did Joseph drive you up?

GRACE. (*Surprised, but recovers quickly.*) Of course. How else would we have gotten there?

JANET. On the train?

GRACE. I didn't say what other conveyances might have been employed to carry us. I meant how else would *we* have gotten there? (*A beat.*) Do you see the difference?

JANET. Would you mind if I talked to Joseph?

GRACE. Joseph is a grown man and is certainly free to speak to whomever he chooses. How could I mind?

JANET. Thank you.

GRACE. But ask yourself one question, will you?

JANET. Of course.

GRACE. If you went to do a story on the governor's wife, would you speak to her chauffeur? (*Enter Marie from upstairs.*)

MARIE. Stop the presses!

JANET. (*Amused.*) That's the first time I ever actually heard anybody say that!

MARIE. I think the world is coming to an end.

GRACE. What are you talking about, Marie?

MARIE. You forgot your pearls.

GRACE. Oh! (*Her hand flies involuntarily to her throat. This is a first and indicates her scattered frame of mind.*)

MARIE. (*She puts the pearls around Grace's neck and does the clasp.*) There! Order has been restored! Gracie will be down in a minute.

JANET. (*Admiring Marie's dress.*) I thought dinner the night I got here was as dressed as people were allowed to be on a week night, but I see I was wrong.

MARIE. I want to thank you for looking at Gracie's stories. She's walking on air.

JANET. She's a good writer. Wise beyond her years.

MARIE. I wish I could say she gets that from me.

JANET. She's also a hopeless romantic.

MARIE. That she definitely gets from me.

JANET. You must be so proud of her for getting into Barnard. Their Creative Writing program is so competitive. If I tried to get in there, even now, they'd probably tell me to mind my manners. *(Marie almost chokes. She hasn't prepared Grace for this yet.)*

GRACE. Barnard?

MARIE. *(Covering quickly.)* Yes, we're all very proud. Gracie applied to several places and was accepted at each one.

GRACE. But she will be starting at Fisk in the fall. *(The bell rings. Jessie admits Catherine.)*

JANET. Oh! I must have misunderstood. I thought she said she was coming to New York.

GRACE. *(Looking at Marie accusingly as Catherine enters the living room.)* The women in our family always go to Fisk.

CATHERINE. And the men go to Meharry! It's tradition. *(She kisses Grace.)* Hello, dearest.

GRACE. Catherine …

CATHERINE. *(A general greeting.)* Everyone! Marie, that dress is more lovely every time I see it.

MARIE. I can't hold a candle to you, Miss Catherine. In fashion and across the board! *(She hugs Catherine encouragingly.)* You always set the standard.

CATHERINE. *(Surprised at this unexpected accolade, but pleased to have it.)* One does what one can.

GRACE. Marie! Why don't you get Miss Logan some more sherry and let me have one quick word with Catherine before our other guests arrive?

MARIE. Of course. Miss Logan?

JANET. Please call me Jan.

MARIE. I keep forgetting! Jan … *(They move to the bar area. We see, but do not hear them talking. As the scene progresses, they sip their sherry and continue to chat, sometimes obviously referencing the family portraits.)*

CATHERINE. I don't think I can go through with it, Grace! I'm a nervous wreck!

GRACE. Of course you can! Here! *(She hands Catherine her sherry which she sips gratefully.)*

CATHERINE. Bless you!

GRACE. Now calm down and let's go over it one more time. Marie and I will go check on dinner and …

CATHERINE. Isn't Jessie cooking?

GRACE. Of course Jessie's cooking.

CATHERINE. Then what is there to check on?

GRACE. *(A beat. She reminds herself to be patient with her flustered friend.)* It's just an excuse to leave you and Miss Jackson alone together so you can get the letter.

CATHERINE. Yes, of course! *(Sips sherry.)* See what I mean? I'm a wreck!

GRACE. You're fine. Once Marie and I leave the room, you give her a glass of sherry the way you would any other guest in my house, and then ask her for it!

CATHERINE. Just like that?

GRACE. She'll give you the letter. You take it, thank her and ask how much she wants for it.

CATHERINE. Should I write it down?

GRACE. No. There won't be time. You'll have to keep it in your head.

CATHERINE. I'll never be able to remember it.

GRACE. Just say it back to her once to get it in your mind. You'll be fine.

CATHERINE. Well, I will, or I won't, I guess. *(She finishes Grace's sherry and hands her the empty glass.)*

GRACE. You will. Now let's get back to the others!

CATHERINE. Wait, Grace! Wait! There's one more thing I want to tell you.

GRACE. Yes?

CATHERINE. *(Reaching into a pocket or small wrist purse.)* The first time Miss Logan wanted to write about us and you just refused to hear her out, I can tell you now, I wanted to wring your neck, but I didn't.

GRACE. A fact for which I am eternally grateful!

CATHERINE. But now that things are working out so well, and she's even staying here at the house, I think I would be a fool not to give my grandson a little nudge in the right direction if the moment presents itself. *(She unfolds her white lace handkerchief and shows Grace the ring.)*

GRACE. Your mother's engagement ring? *(Upstairs, Gracie looks up suddenly. She thinks she hears the bell, jumps up, puts on her shoes, straightens her dress and comes downstairs quickly.)*

CATHERINE. Be prepared! Isn't that what they teach them in the Boy Scouts? *(Enter Gracie from the library stairs, Catherine hurries to hide the ring in her cleavage.)*

GRACIE. I thought I heard the bell. Did Bobby come with you, Mrs. Green?

CATHERINE. He's following behind, but I'm sure he'll be along in a minute. He told me he dropped in on you earlier in the week.

GRACIE. Yes, he did.

CATHERINE. And she's missing him already! I told you, these two!

GRACE. Well, she doesn't need to worry. It's not like he's flying in from New York City. *(Gracie is surprised at this non sequitur, but before she can respond, Marie and Jan reunite the two groups with their conversation already in progress.)*

JANET. I know it's a cliché, but their eyes really do seem to follow you around the room.

GRACE. You've become a real admirer of our portraits.

JANET. The only one I still haven't seen is the one of your husband in the library.

MARIE. I think it's the best of them.

GRACIE. I can take you up now if you'd like to see it before the others get here.

JANET. That would be … *(The bell rings before she can finish her sentence and although Gracie has invited her upstairs, she turns on a dime and almost bumps into Jan as she heads for the door.)*

GRACIE. I'll get it! *(Jessie and Gracie almost collide at the door. Grace and Marie are amazed. No one ever answers the door in this house except Jessie, who beats Gracie to it by inches and opens the door to admit Lillie and Alpha.)*

CATHERINE. *(Sotto voce to Jan.)* She's been on pins and needles waiting for my Bobby to get here. I think there's something in the air!

GRACIE. Come in! Come in! I'm so happy you came. We all are! *(She busily ushers them into the living room, stops, smiles with great delight and announces them)* Here they are!

MARIE. Yes, darling, we can see that.

GRACE. Welcome to my home.

ALPHA. I've been here before, Mrs. Dunbar.

GRACE. *(A beat.)* Of course you have. I was speaking to this lovely young woman I'm assuming is your daughter. I'm Grace Dunbar.

LILLIE. I'm Lillie Campbell Jackson.

GRACE. I always love the passing on of family names. This is Catherine Green.

CATHERINE. Charmed ...

GRACE. My daughter-in-law, Marie, our other guest from New York, Janet Logan, and you've met my granddaughter, Gracie, who seems to have expanded her hostessing duties to include greeting her guests at the door.

ALPHA. Janet Logan? From *The New York Times?*

JANET. Last time I checked.

GRACIE. She's here to cover the cotillion.

ALPHA. Kind of a puff piece for you, isn't it?

JANET. Well, every story has some meat if you know where to look.

MARIE. *(To Lillie.)* Congratulations on your acceptance at Meharry.

LILLIE. Thank you.

MARIE. Come this fall, you and Gracie will be practically neighbors.

GRACIE. A friend of mine says they just opened a Chinese restaurant near the campus. Maybe we can go have dinner there sometime. I'd love to have a chance to use the chopsticks he brought me.

CATHERINE. I don't know how they eat with those things. It just seems so much easier to use a proper knife and fork.

JANET. In China that is a proper knife and fork, Mrs. Green.

CATHERINE. Well, all I'm saying is, I'd probably starve to death.

GRACE. I'm sure you'd figure something out. Gracie, I thought you were going to show Miss Logan the portrait of your grandfather in the library.

GRACIE. Oh! Yes! I'm sorry. *(To Lillie.)* Would you like to see it, too? *(Lillie looks at Alpha.)*

ALPHA. Go ahead. I've seen it. *(Gracie, Lillie and Jan exit to the library. During the following scene we see, but do not hear the three women in the library. Gracie is obviously talking about her grandfather's portrait. Jan also takes a look at the titles of the books. She may pull out a book and look at it, etc. Gracie and Lillie would like to be alone to check in with each other about their surprise, but Jan remains.)*

GRACE. *(Brightly to Alpha.)* Catherine, dear, would you get Miss

Jackson some sherry while Marie and I go check on dinner?

CATHERINE. Oh! Of course. Certainly. *(Grace and Marie exit. Marie gives Catherine a little encouraging pat. Once alone with Alpha, Catherine doesn't move, immobilized by her fear of not executing the plan.)*

ALPHA. *(Tired of waiting, she heads for the bar area.)* I think I can get it myself, thanks.

CATHERINE. Oh! No! Please! Let me get it. Grace will have my head if I let a stranger ... but you're not really a stranger since ... Here, let me get it! *(Catherine is almost babbling as she pours a sherry and hands it to Alpha.)*

ALPHA. Thank you.

CATHERINE. You're welcome. *(They sip in awkward silence. Catherine has no idea how to bring up the letter.)*

ALPHA. I'm sorry your grandson won't be joining us.

CATHERINE. He won't? I thought he was on his way.

ALPHA. *(Surprised.)* On his way here?

CATHERINE. He just needed to change and then he said he was coming right over.

ALPHA. Well, that will be an unexpected pleasure. I've never met your grandson but I understand he and my daughter have had some classes together.

CATHERINE. You've never met him? Then how did you know he wasn't coming?

ALPHA. I must have misunderstood.

CATHERINE. So he is coming?

ALPHA. As far as I know.

CATHERINE. Well, that's a relief.

ALPHA. Glad I could put your mind at ease. *(A beat.)*

CATHERINE. Grace told me ... I'm supposed to ... she said you would know ... if I told you.

ALPHA. *(Thoroughly confused.)* Told me what?

CATHERINE. That I'm the ... that I'm supposed to ... get it from you.

ALPHA. Get what from me?

CATHERINE. *(Sotto voce.)* The letter.

ALPHA. *(Instantly suspicious.)* What letter?

CATHERINE. The one that says ... the one you two talked about earlier.

ALPHA. The one Dr. Dunbar wrote?

74

CATHERINE. Yes! Yes! That's the one. You're supposed to give it to me and I'll give it to Grace.

ALPHA. So you're the go-between?

CATHERINE. No … I'm more a friend who wants to help.

ALPHA. *(Reaches in pocket or purse and takes out the letter in a business envelope. She holds it out to Catherine.)* Good. Then give her this. *(Catherine takes the letter gratefully, turns to go find Grace immediately, then realizes there is one more thing she must do.)*

CATHERINE. *(Turning back to Alpha miserably.)* There is … one more thing. I'm to ask you about … how much … about the … money. About how much money you want for … you know … the letter.

ALPHA. It's not for the letter! That would be blackmail. It's for our pain and suffering.

CATHERINE. Yes, of course it is. Pain and suffering. *(A beat. Alpha glares at her.)* So … how much money are you asking for your … pain and suffering?

ALPHA. Four thousand five hundred and sixteen dollars.

CATHERINE. *(Shocked at the amount.)* Are you sure?

ALPHA. How can you put a price on pain and suffering? *(In the library, Jan says goodbye to the girls and comes downstairs.)*

CATHERINE. You're right, of course. *(Trying to commit the figure to memory.)* Four thousand five hundred and seventeen dollars.

ALPHA. *Sixteen* dollars.

CATHERINE. Oh, isn't that what I said? *(Enter Jan. Catherine, seeing her, wants to hide the letter, but where? She considers her cleavage, but the envelope is too big.)*

JANET. I think Marie is right. It's absolutely beautiful.

CATHERINE. Where is Marie? She and Grace have all but permanently disappeared from our midst!

JANET. *(To Alpha.)* You said you've seen it?

ALPHA. Many times.

JANET. Really? How do you know the Dunbars?

CATHERINE. *(Covering so Jan won't know the truth.)* Montgomery is such a small town, in spite of our sheen of sophistication. Everybody knows everybody else.

ALPHA. My mother was their maid for forty years.

JANET. *(Surprised.)* Oh!

ALPHA. *(Instantly prickly.)* What does that mean? *Oh?*

JANET. Nothing.

CATHERINE. Just think of that? Forty years a maid and now you're here with us for dinner. Who says times aren't changing? More sherry anyone?

ALPHA. My mother was a maid, Mrs. Green. I'm a legal secretary.

JANET. *(Allowing Catherine to refill her glass.)* I guess in forty years your mother and the Dunbars became friends in addition to …

ALPHA. No. They never did …

CATHERINE. *(Increasingly nervous.)* Where could Grace and Marie have gotten off to? Don't they know too many cooks spoil the broth?

ALPHA. But my mother had the greatest respect for Dr. Dunbar.

CATHERINE. Everybody loved him! They really did. Friends, patients, family. Just everybody!

ALPHA. The funny thing is, if you met him and then you met Grace, you'd never put them together.

JANET. Why?

ALPHA. Because he had a heart. *(Catherine who had been feeling fairly relaxed at how things were going, leaps back into the conversation to deflect Jan's attention.)*

CATHERINE. So many changes. Practically makes my head spin. More sherry?

JANET. So, you grew up down here?

ALPHA. I love the way you say *down here* like it's another country.

JANET. Sure looks that way from Harlem.

ALPHA. You got that right.

CATHERINE. I was in Harlem once and I have never seen so many colored people in all my life! Grace had talked me into going to see a Broadway show, but once we got there, nothing would do but we had to go traipsing all over Harlem trying to catch a glimpse of Adam Clayton Powell. Grace swore she admired his politics, but I think she admired his style.

JANET. He sure has enough of both to spare. How long are you in town for?

ALPHA. That depends. *(She looks at Catherine, who gets so nervous, she promptly drops the letter.)*

CATHERINE. Oh, my goodness! *(Jan bends down, picks it up and hands it back to Catherine as the lights go down in the living room. We see Jan and Alpha pour more sherry. Catherine flutters around nervously as we see, but do not hear, Jan and Alpha continuing their conversation. Lights up full on Lillie and Gracie in the library.)*

LILLIE. I'm so nervous. I thought she'd never go back downstairs!

GRACIE. That dress is amazing! I almost didn't recognize you.

LILLIE. Maybe I should go change. I've got my overalls in the trunk of the car.

GRACIE. Overalls? How many times in your life do you think you get to defy convention, challenge authority, break up a perfectly respectable dinner party and then dash off into the night in the arms of your beloved?

LILLIE. I'm guessing two or three, tops.

GRACIE. So do you want to do it in your overalls or in a fabulous, movie star evening dress and a pair of ankle strap high heel shoes?

LILLIE. Maybe Bobby won't recognize me either.

GRACIE. Bobby would recognize you if we put a bag over your head and a pair of clown shoes on your feet!

LILLIE. *(Stopping in front of the portrait.)* What do you think your grandfather would say if he saw us up here plotting a getaway in his library?

GRACIE. I think he'd say, "All's fair in love and war."

LILLIE. He'd be half right. *(A beat.)* How many doctors are in your family?

GRACIE. I don't know. Every generation since the end of slavery, I think.

LILLIE. Didn't you ever want to be one?

GRACIE. I'm not supposed to *be* one. I'm only supposed to *marry* one.

LILLIE. *(Looking at the books with curiosity and admiration.)* My, God, there's a real *Gray's Anatomy* up there!

GRACIE. It was my grandfather's and then my dad's. They would pass it on to the next doctor and then he was supposed to do the same. I guess I kind of broke the chain.

LILLIE. Can I see it?

GRACIE. Sure. *(Gracie pulls over a small stool, stretches to reach the book. She has a hard time reaching it in her dress and when she does, it's so big, she almost drops it. As she catches it, a business envelope drops out and falls behind the couch.)* Good grief! You can't do anything in a dress like this!

LILLIE. You're not supposed to do anything in a dress like that. Didn't your grandmother tell you? *(Gracie hands the book to Lillie and awkwardly tries to retrieve the letter from behind the couch while Lillie touches the book gently.)*

77

GRACIE. *(Still feeling for the letter.)* Did you always want to be a doctor?

LILLIE. Always. *(She's looking through the book as she talks, admiring the plates of the human body, etc. This is a holy book to her.)* When I was about five, this little kid in our building, in the apartment upstairs, got shot in the leg by mistake.

GRACIE. *What?*

LILLIE. His parents were fighting and when my mom heard the shot, and somebody started screaming, she ran upstairs to see if she could help. *(Gracie grabs the envelope from behind the couch, but now she's caught up in the story, so she sits down to listen, ignoring the envelope in her hand.)* I could hear my mother banging on their door and the man was hollering and his wife was screaming and I could hear my mom saying, "You better open this door, you damn fool!" *(Gracie quickly grabs a pen off the desk and starts writing the story on the envelope as Lillie tells it.)*

GRACIE. Go on …

LILLIE. So she busted up into their apartment and it turns out he had been trying to shoot his wife, but he missed and the bullet hit their kid, who had just started walking. Nobody seemed to know what to do next, so my mom grabbed the kid and ran back downstairs, with the mother running right behind her, hollered for me to come on, and we all tumbled out into the snow and started running the two blocks to Harlem Hospital as fast as we could.

GRACIE. *(Writing furiously to keep up.)* What happened when you got there?

LILLIE. My mom started shouting, "I got a kid with a gunshot wound! I got a kid with a gunshot wound!" So much blood was gushing out of his leg, I just knew he was gonna die. *(A beat.)* But he didn't. The doctor cleaned it out, stitched him up, told us he'd be walking just fine again in no time and left. No big fuss. No big fanfare. *(A beat.)* And he was right. That kid never even had a limp. I figured there couldn't be a better job than that.

GRACIE. When your mom ran upstairs, wasn't she scared of getting shot?

LILLIE. My mom isn't scared of anything. *(Lights down in the library. We see the girls talking. Gracie is writing on both sides of the envelope. Lights up full on Alpha, Jan and a very nervous Catherine in the living room as Grace and Marie reenter.)*

CATHERINE. There they are! Thank the Lord for small favors!

GRACE. Well, it's lovely to be missed for such a brief absence.

MARIE. *(Carrying a silver platter with appetizers.)* You will be happy to know that dinner is not far off and in the meantime, Jessie has sent out something warm and wonderful to tide us over.

JANET. It certainly smells wonderful! *(Marie passes the tray to Alpha and Jan. Forgetting her mission, Catherine reaches for an appetizer.)*

GRACE. Catherine, dear, may I see you for just a minute? *(Catherine realizes she's still holding the envelope and quickly joins Grace as far away from the others as possible. We see them enjoying the food, etc.)*

GRACE. Were you going to have hors d'oeuvres?

CATHERINE. Of course not. I'm so nervous, I couldn't possibly eat a morsel. *(She hands Grace the letter.)*

GRACE. *(Half turns her back to Catherine and opens the envelope quickly. She immediately realizes this is a fake.)* This is not the letter.

CATHERINE. That has to be the letter. She handed it to me less than ten minutes ago right over there.

GRACE. I don't care. This cannot be Dunbar's letter!

CATHERINE. How can you be sure?

GRACE. She typed it up herself. But she's not as smart as she thinks she is. *(Shows letter to Catherine.)* She put yesterday's date on it.

CATHERINE. Call the police, Grace! Have them both arrested!

GRACE. And how is that going to play in *The New York Times* society pages?

CATHERINE. But she's lying! She hasn't a shred of evidence.

GRACE. Which won't stop her from telling this story to Miss Logan over dessert and coffee, and then where will we be?

CATHERINE. You're right, you're right! Then what shall we do?

GRACE. How much money did she want?

CATHERINE. You're not going to pay her, are you?

GRACE. I certainly am. *(She's figuring this out as she speaks.)* I'll tell her I have to move some funds around to cover such a large amount and give her a post-dated check. By the time she gets back to New York and tries to cash it, the cotillion will be over, Miss Logan will be out of my house, and I will have alerted the proper authorities. *(She is pleased with this new strategy.)* Now, how much?

CATHERINE. *(Even more confused by this new plan.)* Oh, Lord, Grace, it was a lot. Thousands and thousands of dollars.

GRACE. How much *specifically?*

CATHERINE. Four thousand and … no! That's not it … five

thousand … no! It wasn't that much. *(She's getting further and further from any chance of remembering the figure.)*

GRACE. Sh-h-h! It's all right, Catherine. You're doing fine. Now take a deep breath, close your eyes, don't think about it and just tell me the number … *now!*

CATHERINE. *(Startled into remembering.)* Four thousand five hundred and sixteen dollars!

GRACE. What?

CATHERINE. Oh, Grace, don't make me say it again!

GRACE. Four thousand five hundred and sixteen dollars?

CATHERINE. Yes! That's it exactly!

GRACE. *(Realizing what is going on.)* That's four years' tuition and fees at Meharry.

CATHERINE. How did you know that?

GRACE. I'm on the board, remember? We had to raise tuition at the last board meeting and the sixteen dollars struck me as adding insult to injury, but they insisted. *(A beat.)* She's blackmailing us to pay her daughter's way through medical school.

CATHERINE. The nerve! I'll call the police myself!

GRACE. You'll do no such thing.

CATHERINE. I won't?

GRACE. *(Reaches into her pocket and pulls out a check and a small silver pen. She puts a figure on the check, folds it several times, and hands it to Catherine.)* You'll take this check and discreetly hand it to Miss Jackson.

CATHERINE. *(Folding the check still smaller.)* And then what?

GRACE. Then we can all enjoy our dinner. *(Doorbell rings. In the library, we see Gracie and Lillie hear it, too. They are excited to think Bobby has arrived. Lillie pats her hair nervously. Gracie, still clutching the letter in her hand, cracks the door so they can hear what is going on downstairs. Jessie admits Bobby Green, who keeps his coat, a Casablanca-style trench. He may be carrying a hat. The overall effect should be passionate and dashing.)*

CATHERINE. Oh! Who else is coming? *(During this moment, Catherine drops the small, very folded check. She doesn't notice and neither does Grace.)*

GRACE. Your grandson, dear! *(She goes to greet him.)* Bobby! Your grandmother has been beside herself.

BOBBY. Good evening, Mrs. Dunbar. I'm sorry I'm …

CATHERINE. You're not dressed!

BOBBY. I'm sorry. I do apologize, but I …

MARIE. Bobby, come and meet our other guests, two New Yorkers, visiting with us here in Montgomery.

BOBBY. *(Agitated.)* Yes, well, pleased to meet you. Grandmother, may I speak to you for a just a …

CATHERINE. Don't be rude, dear. You haven't even taken off your coat!

GRACE. Miss Jackson, Miss Logan, Bobby Green, who completes our little group for this evening and who is the king of our centennial ball.

BOBBY. Very nice to meet you. Grandmother, I really need …

JANET. So are congratulations in order?

BOBBY. On being chosen king? It was Gracie's choice. I didn't have to compete for it or anything. If you'll excuse …

JANET. I meant on your engagement. *(Bobby frowns at Catherine.)*

CATHERINE. I haven't said a word! It was in the paper, after all.

BOBBY. *(This is the last thing he wants to hear.)* There is no engagement. *(Alpha is surprised to hear this.)*

JANET. Oh?

BOBBY. Grandmother, may I see you for just a moment, please?

MARIE. Gracie's upstairs in the library, Bobby. She's expecting you.

BOBBY. Thank you. I just need a moment. *(He takes his grandmother's arm and they exit to the foot of the stairs up to the library. They are out of sight of the others whom we see chatting but do not hear. In the library, we also see Gracie put her finger to her lips for Lillie to be quiet as she and Lillie listen to every word that passes between Catherine and Bobby.)*

CATHERINE. I hope you have a good explanation for why you couldn't be bothered to dress for dinner.

BOBBY. Grandmother, you have got to stop trying to run my life. *(Catherine is shocked into silence by the vehemence of his request. She purses her lips and looks away. He softens.)* Please.

CATHERINE. Oh, don't let's fight, Bobby. You've been working so hard, you haven't been yourself. I know that!

BOBBY. *(Gently.)* Grandmother, I am more myself than I have ever been in my life.

CATHERINE. What?

BOBBY. I wasn't going to come here tonight at all. I was just going to leave you a letter or a note or something and hope you would understand. *(In the living room, we see Jan spill something on her sweater. Marie attempts to help her clean if off.)*

CATHERINE. Understand what, dear?

BOBBY. I'm in love, Grandmother. I'm in love with a woman who makes me so happy. I'm going to ask her to marry me.

CATHERINE. *(Thinking he means Gracie.)* Oh, my dearest boy! Nothing would please me, more!

BOBBY. Do you mean it?

CATHERINE. How can you even ask such a thing? Would I have brought this if I didn't mean it? *(She reaches into her cleavage and pulls out the ring she dropped earlier when Gracie made her first entrance. She takes his hand and drops the ring triumphantly into his palm.)*

BOBBY. *(Cringing a little.)* It's warm!

CATHERINE. Of course it is! I've been carrying it around next to my heart all evening just in case you needed it. I have wanted you and Gracie Dunbar to be man and wife since before you were born! *(Jan decides to go upstairs and change quickly. As she moves past the area where Catherine was earlier, she sees the tiny wadded up check. She picks it up, looks at it as she goes upstairs to the second floor.)*

BOBBY. Grandmother, you're still not listening to me! *(Lights down on Bobby and Catherine. Lights up on Marie, Alpha and Grace.)*

MARIE. *(A sudden decision to clear the air.)* I want you to know that I'm very disappointed in you, Miss Jackson.

ALPHA. Disappointed in me?

GRACE. *(Quickly.)* Marie, where are your manners?

MARIE. I'm sorry, Grace, but I just can't sit here and act like I don't know what's going on.

ALPHA. So she told you?

MARIE. Of course she told me. I just don't understand how you can even think about blackmailing Mrs. Green. You should be ashamed!

ALPHA. Mrs. Green?

GRACE. Marie! I've taken care of it!

MARIE. What kind of example are you setting for your daughter?

ALPHA. Leave my daughter out of this!

MARIE. How can I? She's here in this house, just a few feet away from where her mother is engaged in the commission of a terrible crime!

GRACE. This is none of your affair, Marie!

MARIE. Yes it is! Catherine is my friend, too, and even though I'm not pushing for it, her grandson might marry my daughter someday. How can I just sit by and —

ALPHA. Oh, that is rich! You people are absolute fiends, do you know

82

it? Tell me this then, if her grandson is so in love with *your* daughter, why did he spend last summer in Mississippi with *my* daughter?

GRACE. *(Shocked.)* Mississippi?

MARIE. That was *your* daughter? *(Lights up on Bobby and Catherine still on the stairs. He reaches out to take her hands in his in a very gentle, loving gesture.)*

BOBBY. Don't you see, Grandmother? This woman gives a form and a shape to my whole life. She makes me want to be a better doctor and a better man. *(In the library, Gracie and Lillie should react to this joyfully, but silently. Catherine is in shock.)* And all the money and all the houses and all the perfect waltzes and first class trips to Paris don't mean a damn thing if she isn't standing right there beside me, 'til death do us part. *(This almost causes Lillie to swoon with happiness. She and Gracie clasp hands tightly. Jan reenters from the other stairs. As she nears Bobby and Catherine, it is clear they are arguing.)*

CATHERINE. Robert Stephen Green, have you completely lost your ... *(Catherine sees Jan and stops herself in mid-sentence, smiles brightly at Jan who can see there is trouble brewing. She smiles back, sensing a story.)*

JANET. I'm usually allowed to get through the main course before I spill anything. I think this may be a record, even for me. *(A beat. Nobody knows quite what to say.)*

JANET. Everything okay?

CATHERINE. Everything is fine. Just fine.

JANET. Well then, shall we rejoin the others and see how close we are to what I understand is Jessie's world famous standing rib roast?

CATHERINE. *(Wanting to finish her discussion with Bobby but loath to seem as if anything is wrong.)* Yes, of course.

BOBBY. I'm going to say hello to Gracie. We'll be down in a minute. *(In the library, Gracie, hearing this, quickly moves away from the door and motions Lillie to stand in a location providing maximum impact when Bobby walks in the room.)*

CATHERINE. Bobby ... *(He turns away to go up to the library. Catherine turns to Jan and they head back to the group. Bobby knocks softly. Gracie makes him wait while Lillie takes a deep breath, then nods to Gracie: okay. To Jan.)* She swears it's in the marinade. *(As Catherine and Jan rejoin the others, we see Gracie open the library door. Bobby steps into the room. He immediately sees his beloved standing before him in her lovely gown. He thinks she is an angel. She knows*

83

that she is not, but suspects this could be heaven. He runs into her open arms. They share a passionate embrace. Gracie discreetly leaves the room, closes the door, and sits down on the steps as if a sentry. As she sits, she realizes she is still clutching the envelope. She opens it and finds a business letter with a smaller, handwritten note paper clipped to it. Curious, she starts to read and is immediately absorbed. Jan and Catherine rejoin the group as Alpha is saying the following.)

ALPHA. Look! I don't know about all that and I really don't care to discuss it with you Dunbars. All I know is, I gave your friend the letter and now I think you owe me something. *(As they see Jan approaching, all conversation suddenly stops.)*

JANET. *(Grinning at their discomfort. This is the energy on which she thrives.)* I seem to be developing a talent for bringing conversations to a screeching halt, just by entering the room. If I couldn't chalk it up to my chosen profession, my feelings might be hurt.

GRACE. And that would mean I had failed as a hostess, Miss Logan. Let's find a suitable topic so we all can participate. Marie, get Catherine a sherry, will you? You look like you've seen a ghost, dear.

CATHERINE. I do feel rather faint now that you mention it. That grandson of mine will be the death of me yet! *(Marie pours sherry.)*

GRACE. Perhaps you can give us your impressions of Montgomery so far. I'm sure we'd love to hear.

JANET. Well, I can start with — oh! *(Reaches into her pocket, pulls out the check, refolded very small again. She unfolds it as she speaks.)* I found this at the foot of the stairs when I went up to change. *(Grace's face remains impassive, but Catherine's horrified realization that she is responsible for this disaster is unmistakable. Jan doesn't know what she's got yet, but she knows she's got something. Looking at the now fully unfolded check.)* Of course in your spotless house, it jumped out at me and I picked it up intending to drop it in the nearest wastebasket, but something made me unfold it, just to be sure it wasn't something valuable, because how would I know? *(She smiles, waiting for Grace to squirm. Grace is still as a statue.)*

MARIE. What is it?

JANET. It's a check from Mrs. Dunbar, but it's made out to Alpha Campbell Jackson, so I'm not sure to whom I should return it. *(Jan looks at Grace. She thinks she has Grace cornered. A beat. Then Grace looks at Alpha with a huge, rueful smile.)*

GRACE. Well, Miss Jackson, I guess the cat is out of the bag.

84

ALPHA. *(Thrown for a loop.)* I don't ... I don't know what you mean.

GRACE. *(Laughs gaily.)* That must have been why Catherine looked so stricken when the two of you came from the stairway. She must have suspected you knew. Was that it, dear?

CATHERINE. *(Completely confused, can do nothing but agree.)* Yes, Grace. I'm sure that was it.

GRACE. Everyone had been sworn to secrecy, but in the end we're just no match for your investigative skills, are we, Marie?

MARIE. *(Goes along, still thinking she's protecting Catherine.)* Not even close.

GRACE. So, we may as well confess. I release all of you from your oath of secrecy. We had hoped to wait until the ball to make this announcement, but what are a few hours among friends? *(While Grace spins the scholarship yarn, we see Bobby and Lillie tenderly break their embrace and open the library door to find Gracie still sitting there, stunned, the letter still in her hand. She hands the letter up to Lillie, who reads it. Bobby leans over her shoulder to read it, too.)*

JANET. Exactly.

GRACE. Exactly. *(She plucks the check from Jan's hand.)* So it is with great pleasure that I formally bestow the Louis A. Dunbar Scholarship in Medicine upon Miss Lillie Campbell Jackson. *(She hands the check to Alpha.)*

ALPHA. *Bestow?*

JANET. I thought The Nacirema Society doesn't believe in giving scholarships.

GRACE. Oh, that was just my way of trying to throw you off the track of our good intentions. Scholarships are at the very heart of our mission to uplift young Negro womanhood.

JANET. Were you surprised that your daughter was chosen?

ALPHA. I think it's what Dr. Dunbar would have wanted.

GRACE. I'm sure it is.

ALPHA. Then why didn't you just do it?

JANET. Do what?

ALPHA. *(Shares a look with Grace, decides she's had enough and stands up.)* It's been a lovely evening, but I think it's time to say good night.

MARIE. Good night? Aren't you staying for dinner?

ALPHA. I would love to, but I've got a very early flight in the morning. We wouldn't want to wear out our welcome.

JANET. Aren't you even going to tell your daughter she's won so she can thank her benefactor? *(Lillie and Bobby finish reading the letter. They look at each other and share a look with Gracie. All are stunned.)*

ALPHA. *Benefactor?* Is that what you think this is? Some kind of Lady Bountiful stepping up to help the maid's granddaughter? Is that what it looks like to you?

MARIE. I'm sure she didn't mean …

ALPHA. Yes, she did. *(To Grace.)* And so did *she,* but it doesn't matter because my Lillie deserves that money, even if there never was a real scholarship, because she's smart and strong and she's going to be a wonderful doctor, even if her grandfather wasn't named Dunbar!

MARIE. *(To Grace.)* Dunbar? I thought you said …

CATHERINE. *(Sotto voce.)* I thought she wasn't supposed to talk about that anymore.

GRACE. Hush, Catherine!

JANET. Talk about what?

ALPHA. Nothing. If somebody could just get our coats, I'll collect my daughter and … *(Looking at the check for the first time. To Grace.)* What is this?

GRACE. I told you, the first annual Louis A. Dunbar Memorial Scholarship.

ALPHA. Did I ask you for five thousand dollars? *(Hearing the tone in her mother's voice, Lillie hands the letters to Gracie and comes downstairs, holding Bobby's hand. Gracie is behind them. They stand quietly watching as the conversation proceeds. No one is aware that they have come downstairs.)*

GRACE. That is the amount of the award, Miss Jackson.

ALPHA. I asked you for four thousand five hundred and sixteen dollars. No more. No less, but you couldn't even do that without showing off, could you? Without making me feel small. *Oh, no!* You round up and make it an even five grand!

GRACE. Perhaps the recipient might need some clothes …

ALPHA. Clothes? You know what? I wouldn't give you the satisfaction of taking a dime from you. *(She tears up the check and lets the pieces flutter to the floor.)* My daughter and I don't need your money. We are resourceful, hardworking women, something about which you know less than nothing, and I apologize to the memory of my mother forever suggesting she might have mixed our blood with whatever it is that flows in the veins of you Dunbars!

CATHERINE. I think I'm going to faint!

GRACE. Don't you dare! *(Alpha spots the three young people who have been out of sight on the steps come downstairs. Bobby is still holding Lillie's hand.)*

ALPHA. Get your coat, baby. *(She's moving toward the door.)* We're leaving.

LILLIE. Mom! Wait! There's something we have to tell you.

CATHERINE. Bobby, why are you holding that girl's hand?

ALPHA. That girl is my daughter!

LILLIE. Mom! Can you just listen for a minute! *(All are silent again.)* Read the letter, Gracie. Read both of them. *(Gracie looks at Grace who gives her a look that could stop a clock.)*

GRACE. Do you have something that belongs to me, *dear?*

GRACIE. No ... I ... I have something that belongs to Miss Lillie. *(Now that all eyes are upon her, Gracie is a little intimidated. She looks at her mother. Marie, who knows she has been manipulated, looks at Grace and then to her daughter.)*

MARIE. Go on, Gracie. It's okay.

GRACIE. There are two letters. From Granddaddy Dunbar. One typed and a note in his own handwriting.

CATHERINE. *(To Grace, increasingly confused.)* She didn't give me any handwritten note!

JANET. Who?

CATHERINE. *(She points at Alpha.)* Her!

LILLIE. Leave my mother out of this. She's been through enough!

CATHERINE. What about what I've been through?

BOBBY. Come on, Lillie! This doesn't have anything to do with us.

LILLIE. Yes. It does.

BOBBY. All right. *(He puts his arm around Lillie protectively. She lets him.)* Then read it out, kid. And let the chips fall where they may.

GRACIE. *(Clears her throat.)* I'll read the typed one first. "This is to state that I, Louis A. Dunbar, M.D., do solemnly swear and affirm that I am the natural father of one daughter, legally known as Alpha May Campbell, per her mother's wishes, born December 7, 1925. I accept full responsibility for all actions leading up to the conception and birth of this child and have nothing but the highest regard, respect and affection for Mrs. Lillie Campbell, the mother. Please honor any request being made by the bearer of this letter and know that I, or my heirs, will pledge to repay any costs incurred. To wit, I set my hand and seal, this twenty-fourth day of September, 1957."

MARIE. That's the day before he died! *(Jan takes out her notebook and begins making notes, trying to keep up.)*

ALPHA. But that's not the letter I wrote.

MARIE. He never had a chance to mail it!

JANET. Then where did *you* get it?

GRACIE. It fell out of Granddaddy Dunbar's *Gray's Anatomy* when I was showing Lillie.

ALPHA. *(Slowly, dawning.)* You mean, it's real?

GRACE. *(Looks at her and nods slowly. Unable to deny the truth any longer, she's resigned to it.)* Yes.

JANET. So, Dr. Dunbar is your…?

ALPHA. *We're Dunbars?*

JANET. Wait! *(All freeze.)* There's still the other note.

ALPHA. *We're rich? (Gracie looks at her grandmother who doesn't flinch.)*

GRACE. Read it. *(During the reading of this letter, we should see a transformation in Grace. She has suspected that Dr. Dunbar actually loved Lillie, but this is the proof and she is moved by it, in spite of herself.)*

GRACIE. "My dearest love, my most beautiful, Lillie. In the morning, I will mail the attached letter since you have asked me not to bring it. When I'm gone, take it to Hank Graham at the law office and he'll handle everything. I only pray that one day you will make sure our daughter knows the truth. How could I have been so cruel, and so foolish? How could I not have insisted that the choice was mine to make and not yours? How could I have let anything but the fires of hell keep me from your side? I have loved you so long, but not so well. I am a weak and deeply flawed man in all things save the depth of my love for you. If my prayers are answered, we will meet in heaven where I will finally be your devoted husband for all eternity. My most perfect love … always your Louis." *(No one speaks or moves. Gracie looks around and folds up the note and the letter. She directs this to Bobby.)* So there it is. My *other* inheritance. The story of two people who loved each other for a lifetime and never had the nerve to say it out loud. *(Bobby looks at Lillie. Catherine looks at Bobby.)*

BOBBY. *(To Lillie.)* But it doesn't have to be that way.

LILLIE. Are you sure? *(Bobby reaches in his pocket and pulls out the*

ring Catherine gave him to give to Gracie.)
CATHERINE. *(Realizing what he is about to do.)* Bobby, don't!
MARIE. Catherine, hush!
BOBBY. *(A sudden fear as he opens his mouth to propose. He turns to Alpha.)* You're not related to the Greens, are you?
ALPHA. Not that I know of.
BOBBY. Good. *(Taking Lillie's hand and sliding the ring on her finger.)* Lillie Campbell Jackson, will you do me the indescribable honor of becoming my wife?
LILLIE. Yes, Robert Stephen Green, the third, I will! *(Bobby and Lillie embrace. Catherine faints. Black.)*

Scene 5

In the darkness, we hear the joyful strains of a song like Marvin Gaye's "Pride and Joy."* Lights up on a celebration taking shape in Grace's living room. Present are Alpha, Marie, Janet, Lillie, Bobby, Gracie and Jessie, still in uniform. There is no immediate dialogue but they are all active in the scene. Jessie is passing out champagne in lovely crystal flutes on a silver tray. She serves Alpha, then Marie, who toasts Alpha who is still a little shocked. She serves Bobby and Lillie, offers one to Gracie, who checks with Marie, who nods that it's okay. Lillie, Bobby and Gracie toast happily.

Jan is in a chair, scribbling notes. When Jessie offers her champagne, she stops, looks at her notes, then closes the notebook, puts it down, and accepts the champagne. Marie raises a glass to Jan who returns it with a grin that says: Nobody will believe this anyway. Unseen by Jan, Jessie picks up the notebook and puts it in her pocket. Marie goes to Jan and they talk. Bobby talks happily with Gracie. Lillie sees Jessie standing by with more champagne on a tray beside her. Lillie goes to Jessie, picks up a glass and offers it. Jessie hesitates just a moment, then smiles and accepts it. Lillie and Jessie toast and Jessie becomes a part of the celebration, too.

---

* See Special Note on Songs and Recordings on copyright page.

In the library, we see Catherine lying on the sofa with her feet up and a cool cloth across her eyes. Grace is sitting in a chair beside her, holding her hand. Music out as Catherine slowly removes the cloth from her eyes and looks at Grace.

GRACE. Feeling better?

CATHERINE. I feel ridiculous. *(She sits up slowly with Grace's help. They look at each other.)* I don't know which is worse. That her grandmother was a maid or that her grandfather was your husband.

GRACE. Is that why you fainted?

CATHERINE. What else could I do? I had to buy some time.

GRACE. Time for what?

CATHERINE. For us to figure this out! To make sure these hellions come to their senses.

GRACE. Or we'll cut them off without a penny?

CATHERINE. Exactly!

GRACE. I don't think they care, Catherine.

CATHERINE. Of course they care. You've been in love, but it never made you act a fool.

GRACE. Dunbar was a good man and an amazing doctor and I always respected him, but there was never a spark between us. Not even in the beginning. *(A beat.)* I never held it against him. He kept up his end of our bargain and so did I, and that was always enough for me, so I could pretend it was enough for him. But I always knew it wasn't. *(A beat.)* Dunbar didn't fall in love with Lillie to hurt me. Dunbar just fell in love with Lillie.

CATHERINE. Do you really think he loved her?

GRACE. *(A beat. She knows he did.)* Well, she made him write a beautiful love letter. Maybe his granddaughter can do that for your grandson. And that wouldn't be the worst thing that could happen to him, would it?

CATHERINE. No, I guess it wouldn't. *(Grace reaches for her hand and squeezes it.)* So now what?

GRACE. So now we go downstairs and apologize to my granddaughter for our bad behavior and say welcome to the family.

CATHERINE. *(Groans.)* Why don't you keep sherry up here? You really should. *(Downstairs we see Lillie get a glass of sherry and head up to the library.)*

GRACE. Look on the bright side, my dearest friend. This will still be the generation where our bloodlines mix, even if it is once removed. *(Lillie knocks on the door which is cracked a little and sticks her head in tentatively.)*

GRACE. Come in, dear.

LILLIE. I just wanted to check on Miss Catherine. I thought she might like some … *(Catherine takes the sherry before Lillie can finish the offer.)*

CATHERINE. Bless you!

GRACE. I understand you were looking through Dr. Dunbar's *Gray's Anatomy* today.

LILLIE. Gracie said it was all right. Of course, we didn't have any idea that … *(She stops, not sure how to proceed with these new relationships.)*

GRACE. I want you to have it.

LILLIE. Oh, I couldn't!

GRACE. And so does your grandfather. *(She hands it to her. Lillie accepts it.)* Welcome to the family, dear. *(They embrace.)*

CATHERINE. That's what I was going to say!

GRACE. Then say it.

CATHERINE. Welcome to the family, dear. *(They embrace.)*

GRACE. If we don't get down there soon, they're going to send a search party for us. *(To Catherine.)* Ready, dearest?

CATHERINE. *(Patting her hair, her dress, etc.)* I'm a wreck!

LILLIE. You look beautiful.

CATHERINE. *(Pleased.)* Well, thank you, dear. *(Takes her arm.)* Now what is this about you two going to Mississippi? *(Catherine and Lillie exit downstairs, music up: a song like "Pride and Joy."* Grace remains behind. We see: Bobby and Catherine embrace. Alpha and Lillie embrace. With just a slight shudder, even Alpha and Catherine embrace. Marie and Jessie serve more champagne. Gracie goes to the library stairs looking for her grandmother.)*

JANET. I seem to have misplaced my notes.

MARIE. I'm sure they're around here somewhere.

JANET. Well, it doesn't matter. Nobody would believe this anyway. *(Grace, exiting the library, stops to look back at the portrait of Dr. Dunbar. All is forgiven between them. She turns around to see Gracie waiting for her.)*

---

* See Special Note on Songs and Recordings on copyright page.

GRACE. *(A beat.)* I'm going to miss you all the way up there in New York City.

GRACIE. You can come and visit me.

GRACE. Only when I'm invited. *(Leaving the library door open so that Dr. Dunbar can be part of the celebration, Grace takes Gracie's arm as they join the others.)*

GRACIE. Will you kill me if I write about all this?

GRACE. Absolutely. *(Music up full as they join the others in celebration.)*

End of Play

PROPERTY LIST

Polaroid camera, snapshots
Coffee pot, cup
Newspaper, glasses
Scissors, thumbtack
Small notebook, pen (Grace)
Sherry decanter, glasses
Coats
Notebook (Gracie)
Chopsicks tied with a ribbon
Handbag with: souvenir NYC handkerchief, cosmetics bag, small
    notebook, pens, Doublemint gum, wallet, small New Testament
Small black envelope handbag
Backpack
Typewritten manuscript
White lace handkerchief
Small suitcase
Small locked box with key
Letter on legal pad paper
Purse, reporters notebook, pen
Coffee on silver tray
Typewriter, paper, eraser
Homework
Shopping bags
Evening dress
Handkerchief and engagement ring
Letter in business envelope
Gray's Anatomy and letter in business envelope
Silver platter with appetizers
Checkbook, small silver pen
Trench coat, hat
Silver tray with champagne in crystal flutes
Cool cloth

SOUND EFFECTS

Doorbell
Key in door
Typewriter noise
Pebbles thrown against window
Motown music